RECALCULATING

RECALCULATING

CHARLES BERNSTEIN

THE UNIVERSITY OF CHICAGO PRESS

CHICAGO & LONDON

CHARLES BERNSTEIN

lives in New York and is the Donald T. Regan Professor of English and
Comparative Literature at the University of Pennsylvania, as well as
coeditor of *L=A=N=G=U=A=G=E*, the Electronic Poetry Center, and
PennSound, and cofounder of the SUNY-Buffalo Poetics Program. He is
a fellow of the American Academy of Arts and Sciences. Among his many
publications are three books also published by the University of Chi-
cago Press: *Girly Man*, *With Strings*, and *My Way: Speeches and Poems*.

////////////////////////////////

THE UNIVERSITY OF CHICAGO PRESS, CHICAGO 60637
THE UNIVERSITY OF CHICAGO PRESS, LTD., LONDON
© 2013 BY CHARLES BERNSTEIN
ALL RIGHTS RESERVED. PUBLISHED 2013.
Printed in the United States of America

22 21 20 19 18 17 16 15 14 13   1 2 3 4 5

ISBN-13: 978-0-226-92528-8 (cloth)
ISBN-13: 978-0-226-92530-1 (e-book)

Library of Congress Cataloging-in-Publication Data

Bernstein, Charles, 1950–
Recalculating / Charles Bernstein.
pages. cm.
Includes bibliographical references.
ISBN 978-0-226-92528-8 (cloth : alk. paper)
ISBN 978-0-226-92530-1 (e-book)
I. Title.
PS3552.E7327R43 2013
811'.54—dc23   2012026200

⊗ This paper meets the requirements of
ANSI/NISO Z39.48-1992 (Permanence of Paper).

It is our privilege alone
to disappear
to never forget that we do,
never forget to set down what must be set down
so that it not be forgotten,
not be lost in all this time:
Emma.

Bob Perelman

In darkness let me dwell, the ground shall sorrow be,
The roof despair to bar all cheerful light from me,
The walls of marble black that moisten'd still shall weep,
My music hellish jarring sounds, to banish friendly sleep.
Thus wedded to my woes, and bedded to my tomb,
O, let me, living, living, die, till death do come.

John Dowland

See sun, and think shadow.

Louis Zukofsky

I navigate now without authority. Turn, great sun,
            your disc upon me
        I set out now
        in a box upon the sea

Charles Olson

CONTENTS

The road tells you what to do. Throw on some shades,
pump up the radio, put your hands on the wheel.
Retrace your route in reflection, but look only as far
as the blur of passing yellow lines to see the present.
Race your future to the finish line.

//

EMMA BEE BERNSTEIN

RECALCULATING

////////////////////////////////////

AUTOPSYCHOGRAPHIA

after Fernando Pessoa

Poets are fakers
Whose faking is so real
They even fake the pain
They truly feel
And for those of us so well read
Those read pains feel O, so swell
Not the poets' double header
But the not of the neither
And so the wheels go whack
Ensnaring our logical part
In the train wreck
Called the human heart

1 April 1931

THE TRUTH IN PUDDING

Imagine poetry as a series of terraces, some vast, some no bigger than a pinprick, overlooking the city of language. The sound and light show begins in the dark: sentences dart by, one by one, forming wave after wave of the rag and bone shop of the quotidian, events passing before our eyes like the faint glimmer of consciousness in an alcoholic stupor. Facts, facts everywhere but not a drop to drink.

Now it is dawn, now night, now noon, now morning. It's as if the day never ends, it just keeps coming back for more.

Language is an event of the world, just as, for language users, the world is an event of language. Even the world is a word.

Speak truth to truth.

In the viscosity of process, the end never arrives.

Poetry shows the ink the way out of the inkbottle.

Don't let the Proper Name horse lead the active thinking cart.

A thing of beauty is annoyed forever.

Poetry's social function is not to express but rather to explore the possibilities for expression.

Poetry is difficulty that stays difficult.
[Hank Lazer via Pound / Williams]

Slivers of reason make amends.

Connect the knots.

Blaming others for your own failings is inevitable; getting others to do it for you is unforgivable.

Fate makes us who we are
Just as we make it what it is
But the sadness overwhelms

I don't want interdisciplinarity but nondisciplinarity.

Something there is that doesn't love a frame
That wants it laid bare.

Before I made a frame I'd ask to know
What I was framing in or framing out.

Two frames diverged on the common road
& I, I could not choose the one for the other
So stood, astounded, in place.

For frames are what we are inside of.

Two frames are better than one
Three's the thicket.

Today I am worried about Professor B, who worries about whether his worrying is run-of-the-mill worry or worrisome worry, and this worrying about his worry worries him the most, turning his worrying into the kind of worrisome worry he worries about.

"Is the best you can do really the best you can do?"

Does the work frame the interpretation or the interpretation frame the text? Or is a text a work without a frame?

Poetry starts in the present but immediately takes you to its many pasts, through its many paths.

What is missing from bird's-eye view is plain to see on the ground.

Not incoherent, coherent by other means. By any means necessary.

Not the flow of consciousness but the flow of perception.

"It is not a thought, finished and complete, that seeks expression in a beautiful form. It is thought's struggle, what is in and below the thoughts; it is the things and all things behind them, the life-material, expressed in our perception, that we should render in aesthetic creation."

[Gunnar Bjorling, tr. Fredrik Hertzberg]

What's the difference between narrative and story? What's the difference between stories told and untold? What's the difference between a story told once, a story told twice, and a story told many times? Does a story have to find its own way of telling itself or does the teller tell it? How can you tell the told from the tale?

A fact is a frozen state of affairs. If I had to stipulate the facts of the poem, I would say there are no facts other than the words, and the words are not facts at all but what makes facts possible. The poem is the fact of its own making. The poet is the extension of the fact of the poem.

"It is what it is. It swings."

[Paul Anka]

In the 1990s, it was common in Russia to find stores with empty shelves, but one was stripped to bare walls. It was a shelf store.

So much depends on what you mean by failure, what you want from success, and what you imagine poems do. Insofar as a poem is successful, it fails to fail, but, in failing to fail, it also succeeds at failing. That's a lose-lose scenario (which in the alchemy of poetry we imagine as win-win).

Some praise the beauty of a poem and the exactness of its images. Maybe this is what least I like. The poem's polish makes a glossy surface in which I see myself staring, barred from making it to the other side. Here we find the hymen of voyeurism intact. So here the poetics is compulsory autoeroticism. I have several names for what went wrong: tone constrained, ending boned, syntax pulled thin over box-like frame, then teaspoon used for stirring in feeling.

Either you have talent or we'll buy you some.

Better a four-legged dog than a three-legged cat.

The time is not far off, or maybe it has already come to pass, when computers will be able to write better poems than we can. So we must now add to logopoeia, phanopoeia, and melopoeia: *algorhythmia.*

Good poets make analogies; great poets make analogies between analogies.

Computers will never replace poets because computers won't take that much abuse.

Is the diachronic robustness more valuable than synchronic flickering?

The work of art always exceeds its material embodiment as well as its ideal form: physical or digital instantiations, anterior codes or algorithms, experience while reading or viewing, interpretations, contexts of publication or appearance, historical connections—all these have an affinity, clustering around an empty center.

Three types of fragmentation, or three aspects of any fragment: disjunction, ellipsis, constellation.

Serial frames, each displacing but not replacing one another.

In modular or serial essay form, each of the interchanging parts relate tangentially to the next, forming a cluster around a projected but unstated series of possible motifs. In this way, different aspects of the imaginary are addressed, as if they were the interlocking faces on the surface of a crystal.

Juxtaposing disparate, if related, material forms an array or constellation within an environment.

"We attain to but brief and indeterminate glimpses."
[E. A. Poe, *The Poetic Principle*]

Words falter then fail, love and care persist.
Love falls away, cares betrayed, words remain.

Better last night's salami than this morning's baloney.

Are poetry and poetics at odds? Are poetics and scholarship opposing? Is innovation a matter of aesthetics or of applied research?

Poetry is to the classroom what a body is to a cemetery.

Poetics and innovation are the Scylla and Charybdis, or possibly Mutt and Jeff, or then again dog and bone, or possibly singer and song, or is it doctor and patient, or inner and outer, or hook, line, and sinker?, of the politics of poetic form.

If reading poetry is not directed to the goal of deciphering a fixed, graspable meaning, but rather encourages performing and responding to overlapping meanings, then difficulty is transformed from obstacle to opening.

"It is a puzzle. I am not puzzled but it is a puzzle. . . . I am not puzzled but it is very puzzling."

[Gertrude Stein, *The Mother of Us All*]

everybody talks about the fall of the humanities
but few make the effort to get up.
in other words, does the past have a future?

"The ladder urges us beyond ourselves. Hence its importance. But in a void, where do we place it?"

[Edmond Jabès, tr. Rosmarie Waldrop]

Information is born free but everywhere in chains.

Poetry is metadata without code, free-base tagging, cascading style sheets with undefined markers.

The role of teaching poetry, or of poetry criticism, is not to overrule difficulty, as in a court of law, but to sustain it—to recognize the ways that resistance to easy assimilation might sustain our engagement with the poem and in the process provide aesthetic pleasure and intellectual challenge.

Are we scholars and teachers and artists or academetricians?

The crucial distinction, in our poetics, is not only between presenting and representing, enacting and expressing, but also grasping and pointing.

All poetics is political
All poetry is politics
All politics is poetics

What you think and $5 will get you exactly something that's worth $2.95.

Think of poetry groupings not as islands but as directions: northern or southern, open to inhabitation by different times, different populations.

Schools are made to be broken.

No where to go but on.

Yes, we have no ideology, yes we have no ideology today.

Tumble, sunder, fake, fall. These are not only my subjects but also practice (makes imperfect). Does the poem allow its error to lead? rupture? collapse? rapture?

Even the Pacific Ocean has a bottom, but you'd be hard pressed to get there with even strokes.

I may be wrong, in fact I most surely am wrong, just not as wrong as you.

Two rights almost always make a wrong.

The absence of absence is not evidence of absence. (The evidence of absence is not the absence of evidence.)

What is after me is also after me. I hide in my past.

"But the world will never weary of watching that troubled soul in its progress from darkness to darkness."
[Oscar Wilde, *The Critic as Artist*]

Don't tell me it's time to go to bed because I just woke up.

In Portuguese, you don't count the last syllable.

As if poetry was something you give to your mother-in-law when she goes deaf.

Rabbi Eliza would always say, *Which comes first, the egg or the idea?* as a way to stop a conversation she felt was coming too soon to a conclusion. One very hot afternoon, Rabbi Omar asked Rabbi Eliza to trace the origins of her favorite maxim. "In a roundabout way," Rabbi Eliza began, looking up from the passage she was studying, "it's related to Rabbi Yukel's so-called Rule of the Index Finger: *Don't put all your chickens in one egg,* which itself is a variant of the saying, attributed to Rabbi Raj, and which we chant on the first half moon of winter, *One egg is not the world.* On hearing this, Rabbi Omar loudly protested, noting that several centuries before Rabbi Raj, Rabbi Not-Enough-Sand-in-the-Desert-Not-Enough-Water-in-the-Sea had insisted that the central question to ponder on nights-without-visible-rainbows is, *Which comes first the basket or the idea of the basket?* "Exactly," Rabbi Eliza said with a triumphant laugh, "without baskets or eggs we would only have words and without words only mouths."

Imagine poetry as a series of terraces, some vast, some no bigger than a pinprick, overlooking the city of language. The sound and light show begins in the dark: sentences dart by, one by one, forming wave after wave of the rag and bone shop of the quotidian, events passing before our eyes like the faint glimmer of consciousness in an alcoholic stupor. Facts, facts everywhere but not a drop to drink.

Now it is dawn, now night, now noon, now morning. It's as if the day never ends, it just keeps coming back for more.

Language is an event of the world, just as, for language users, the world is an event of language. Even the world is a word.

POEM LOADING . . .

please wait

TALK TO ME

I have an announcement.

Due to previous engagements
I'm unable to appear tonight
and . . . I will be . . .
replacing myself.
I'm very sorry
but the program is called
"Impulsive Behavior"
so I think we have to make some
changes. Now there's
supposed to be a dialogue
with Bruce Andrews
and Edwin Torres. Had I
been present I might
have joined the
dialogue with Bruce
and Edwin.

But then me . . . me . . .

I don't want to have a dialogue.

That's why
though I'm calling this
Talk to Me
I really would prefer to

talk to myself.

What are you saying?

I can't H E A R you.
BE QUIET!

I want to hear what you're saying—
but I'm not listening!

A poet
Taking a long walk on the ice
Slipped
And fell down.
A critic came along
Seeing him lying there and said
Are you comfortable?
—I make a good living.

I told my wife
I was losing my grip.
She said,
What grip?

My wife she stood—
With a loaded gun—
Who said that?

I've always loved Sally Silvers' work
especially her early work where
she does stuff with movement that's extremely awkward
a kind of awk-
wardness that you don't
associate with dancers.
I always wanted
to do something like that
with poetry
to make poetry almost
painfully
clumsy, clumpsy . . .

perhaps not reciting poems but
declammering poetry
á la Huntz Hall and the Bowery Boys—

How beauteous is—
The subway—
In which I—toil—
Schmutzing my way to the midnight's—
Ball—
Right by where—
You are—

But the problem with that—what?—text
is that the kinds of things I most readily come up with
seem to
follow some kind of
pattern that's
feeding on memory

and the beauty of the
alphabet
of writing it down
is the memory function

it remembers for me

In many ways the in-process writing through poetry is contained in
the performance of poetry, the different ways in which
a relatively fixed alphabetic work

is said differently, is performed

differently.

But the kind of patterns
that I can improvise

don't allow for the kind of
immemorability
which I've always wanted for poetry—

to articulate things
that can't be
remembered
which might mean
phrases
I can't quite
make up
in real time.

It was Alfred Lord and Milman Parry
in their book *The Singer of Songs*
that talked about formulas
of memorized texts

that were especially popular in Greece before the time of the
    alphabet
and continue in cultures after that time
that didn't use writing as a method of memory. Still I want to try
to do a
paperless poem
part of the paperless culture that we're entering into
and see what I can come up with.

Transient

Failure

I'm not telling you
what you CAN'T do,
but what you CAN do.

The pricks are points
on a map.
The past
passes
if we
listen
not
to what it tells but to the tales we tell
about
it—

what time is it NOW what TIME is it now what time is it NOW
what time IS it now WHAT time is it n-o-w what TIME is
it now what time is it *now* what time is it now what TIME is it
NOW what time IS it *now* WHAT TIME IS IT *NOW* what
time is it NOW what time is it now what TIME is it now

the trees

turn
dark

but the leaves are

shot

with light.

Go back! Stay back! Way back!
In back! Kneel back!
Quickback!
Stayback!

Halt! Kick!

Is performance better than writing?
Writing better than Starbucks?
Starbucks better than bugles?
Humor better than seriousness?
Peace
better than tranquility?
Microphone
better than illusion?
Illusion
better than banisters?
Banisters better than walls, ceilings
better than lights, lights
better than trees, trees better than floors, floors
better than what's under the floors?

The warlords
Drank
Blood
From cups
Made of Euro bones

And Euro dollars

And Euro horns

What time is it now? What time is it NOW? What TIME is
it NOW? WHAT time IS IT now? WHAT TIME IS IT
NOW? WHAT TIME IS IT NOW? WHAT TIME IS
IT NOW? What time is it now? WHAT TIME IS IT NOW?
WHAT TIME IS IT NOW? WHAT TIME IS IT NOW?
WHAT TIME IS IT NOW? WHAT TIME IS IT NOW?

[talking watch:]
It's nine eighteen p.m.
It's nine eighteen p.m.
It's nine eighteen p.m.

The light
spills
into pools
of darkness

I cannot
find it

—Now
those are
some of the elements
that might go
into a poem
but in a poem I'd
disperse and
reorganize them
in a way
that would not
have the same
kind of, kind
of rhythmic
structure
that I fall into
when improvising

What time is it now?
TALK to me!
I don't wanna hear what you're saying!
SHUT UP!

What do you think about?

I don't wanna know.

Some of the images are occurring because
one of the people that I'm in dialogue with

is Dubravka Djurić
a Yugoslavian poet and translator
who lives in Belgrade.
And all through this time we've been sending
Internet messages back and forth.
But just before
the recent NATO bombing of Belgrade began
she asked me a question
about a line from Robert Duncan.

And the line was:

The African princes
drink
from cups of rhino bones and horns

. . . and she didn't know what that meant.
And so she sent me an email.
And I thought it was very interesting
in the midst of all that was going on
that she was so concerned what this image
what this poem, of this
poet no longer alive, Robert Duncan,
could mean. And it reminded me of a trip
that James Sherry and I took
to Belgrade in 1991. We rented a car
in Vienna. And drove down to Belgrade.
And then that little tiny car
(James will remember this) . . .
I couldn't get the reverse clutch to work.
And this was extremely irritating
to James, because it wouldn't back up.
We were in a parking space and yet
we couldn't get out of there. I just
couldn't get that clutch to work.

And one thing that Dubravka said to me
somewhere during the Serbo-Croatian war
was that the kind of concern for poetry
and the politics of poetic form that Bruce
was engaged in that I was engaged with
and many others—
took on an acute meaning to her
when that war took place and she never
understood so well why we saw poetics
as political, about what we *can't* think
as much as what we can . . .
worrying about what images mean
how language works
how representation works . . .
it's all very frivolous and fun
but it's not
serious, it doesn't matter but suddenly
it started to matter to her.
One of the reasons it mattered to her was—

What time is it?

DON'TALKTOMEICANTHEARYOU

One of the reasons . . .

DON'TALKTOME

I want to hear you

DON'T TALK TO ME I WANNA HEAR YOU!

One of the reasons was—

. . . you know whenever I want to hear other voices

I have a very
comforting thing. . . .
My watch comforts me.
Talking to other people is OK but
really I only want to hear the dialogue
that I create myself.
That's the problem with poetry:
I want other voices
but I want them always to be

My own other voice

What time is it now?

[talking watch:]
Nine twenty-three p.m.

What time is it now?

It's nine twenty-three p.m.

I find that very comforting
because it answers me. . . .

And I know what the answer's going to be
yet it's still another voice.

Dubravka's mother is from Croatia and her father is from Serbia
so she's a Yugoslavian.
And one of the things that you realize
is that this constant representation of land and a people
in terms of these ethnic maps that we draw . . .

The pricks are points on a map
the points are pricks on a map

There's nothing to lose
but nothing itself
the *thought* of nothing.

Go BACK STAY back WAY back!

Ich bin ein Yugoslavian.

I am a Yugoslavian.

Because, as Dubravka says, the intersections of the different
representations, the ability to live with ambiguity, the ability to live
in dialogue with multiplicity instead of trying to have some moral
order that says this is this sector, that is this sector, everything is
separate, everything is divided . . .

And we're writing together, we're
getting back these messages that say
"transient failure." Transient
failure. As the bombs are falling and then
she writes urgently, she says very urgently
Don't post the message to the listserv
electronic group because I'm afraid
with this message. And what this message says is
before the fall of Communism, there were poets
who were Communist poets, who were all about the Communist
credo, who put forward socialist realist values. And then
in the time of Milosevic there were extreme Serbian nationalist poets . . .
and she didn't want us to post this information . . .
and then . . .
James got a message that said . . .
"fatal error" . . . and I kept thinking what is that?
Fatal error. Transient error. Which one is the fatal error
and which is the transient error? And then I thought
Alfred Lord, *Singer of Tales,* I mean that's a Serbian singer

23

and when you think about improvisation, and oral culture, one of
    the key
ways that we know about it is through the singers of Serbia
and who are *they*? And can we live with a dialogic reality
that doesn't have a fixed order . . . that this is here, and this is there . . .
that there isn't a right or wrong?

Ich bin ein Yugoslavian.

What time is it *now*?
What time is it NOW?
What time is it NOW?

And then we got a message
via B92, which is the alternative radio station
that was shut down on April second
by Milosevic and it said
Don't send any more messages
these messages you're sending are going through the server
and you've got to stop.

Transient error. Fatal error.
We didn't know which.
Could it be a transient error?
Was it going to be fatal?

And I keep thinking of not being able to go into reverse because you
can't go into reverse, you can't go back, and we kept going forward
and I kept thinking maybe talking about this maybe thinking
about the way we talk about things *is* political, *is* crucial and maybe
dialogue is the problem.

Listen—

if we don't have dialogue
if we don't listen to what we *can't* hear
what we *can't* understand
then we're not—

What time is it now?

[talking watch:]
It's nine twenty-seven p.m.
It's nine twenty-seven p.m.

And the curious thing
that Dubravka said
was that these Communist
social realist poets
and the ultra
right-wing poets
the ultra-nationalist poets of the present . . .

they were the same poets.

I'm not telling you
what you *can't* do,
but what you *can* do.

The pricks are points of light
On a map.

The leaves are dark

Before the trees

Are shot with light

GO back STAY back WAY back!

In back! Lay back!

What time is it now? WHAT TIME
is it now? *What time is it **now**?* What
time is it . . . TALK to me! *Talk* to me!
I don't want to hear it. Talk to me
I don't want to hear it! Talk to me
I CAN'T HEAR WHAT YOU'RE
SAYING! *Talk to me.* Be QUIET!

You can't go in reverse.

Fatal error.

Transient error.

And B92's motto,
which they have on their website,
is *Don't trust anybody. Including us.*

TALK to me. *I don't want to hear it!*
What do you think? I'M NOT LISTENING.

They were the same poets.

And you might answer B92's motto:
Don't trust yourself either.

The warlords
Are drinking blood
From cups of Euro bone and Euro horn.

The light

Spills
Into pools

Of darkness.

I cannot find it

By myself.

I've been given a body. What should I do with it,
So singular, so my own?

For this joy, quiet, to live and breathe,
Who, tell me, am I to thank?

I am gardener, but flower too;
In the world's dungeon I am not alone.

On the windowpanes of eternity,
My breath, my warmth has already settled.

On it a pattern is pressed,
Unrecognizable of late.

Even if moment's gloom streams down—
The pattern, so dear, won't be crossed out!

1909

Osip Mandelstam
translated with Kevin Platt

[handwritten annotations: "speaker's not recognizing", "listen", "& charles B."]

SANE AS TUGGED VAT, YOUR LOVE

after Leevi Lehto, "Sanat Tulevat Yolla"

O when sanity tasted of muffled curtsy.
Talon—Jokasta's vivisected valor.
Silly virtual item.
Sane as tugged vat, your love, kaput.

Tamed tapestry's caressed master's tasseled luaus.
O when sanity tasted of muffled curtsy.
Talon—Jokasta's vivisected valor.
Silly virtual item.

Medusa pouts as vat's veil's oldest lament jokes.
Tamed tapestry's caressed master's tasseled luaus.
O when sanity tasted of muffled curtsy.
Talon—Jokasta's vivisected valor.

President—he itsy, oily, tainted, laminated.
Medusa pouts as vat's veil's oldest lament jokes.
Tamed tapestry's caressed master's tasseled luaus.
O when sanity tasted of muffled curtsy.

Talon—Jokasta's vivisected valor.
Silly virtual item, yah!
Sane as tugged vat, your love, kaput.

\ funny

Re-
demption
comes
&
redemp-
tion
goes
but
trans-
ience
is
here
for-
ever.

SAD BOY'S SAD BOY

after "Mad Girl's Love Song" by Sylvia Plath

I ruin my hats and all the mat slides glad
I hop my girls and all is skip again
I jump I run you up inside my truck

The car goes looping out in dark and light
And yellow hat slides in
I run my mats and all the girl slides glad

I hoped you skipped me into luck
And jump me black, ruin me glad
I jump I run you up inside my truck

I jump my slopes and all the dopes slide glad
I glide my luck and all is slip again
I jump my hopes and all the rope glides sad

I skip you jump the way you said
But I run old and sigh your name
I ruin my mats and all the girl slides glad

At least when luck hops it skips back again
A rune my mats and all the girls slide glad
I jump I run you up inside my truck

DESIGN

for Jean-Michel Rabaté

I saw the sign
on its hooks
grappling with
the being of its
having become &
gone, in a flash
just like the gun
returned to its holster
or the prairie dog
howling with
homesickness
even at home.
The consciousness of
consciousness lapses
into intermittent
power outages &
salt water taffy.
History will end
& the sooner
the better
as long as
I have my
season pass.

BLUE TILE

My pa & mine ma
dead
no ones
some

one
double
silence
uninterrupted

jagged shards
that, now,
by act of accumulation
I rejoin

Régis Bonvicino, "Azulejo" (2007)

THE HONOR OF VIRTUE

What I say is what I meant
& what I saw is what I said
But neither seen nor spoke
Is what I think I thought

BLOWN WIND

after Douglas Messerli

Slow pain's

lust of facts

quickens transport

into earth

quake and bolt against

temptation to, from

certain

flicker of

as rock rattles

rhythm, sentiments

sediment

to snare

despair.

THE DUCK HUNTERS

for Ernesto Livon-Grosman

"I remember beautiful rivers
but not the boat to take you there." *Antigone?*

The shots ring across Plaza de Mayo
16 June 1955. Even
the duck hunters shudder at blood-splattered
column of Cristoforo Colombo,
rising up upon the shoulders of those   *civil
disobedience*
from before. While we are now, or nearly
now. "Those who use violence against their
enemies will, turning, use violence
against themselves, even their own people."
Dulce de leche but the memory
slashes. Go back, daylight too hard to bear,
night soaks in despair. No moment exists
save this one, doubling over heave & mar
& spill, in still more furious repair.

Buenos Aires, 16 June 2005

On June 16, 1955, Argentine navy planes bombed the gov-
ernment and cultural center of Buenos Aires in an attempt
to kill the elected president, Juan Peron. The pope had ex-
communicated Peron on the same day. After three hundred
unarmed civilians died in the attack, a crowd torched the
nearby Buenos Aires cathedral. The epigraph is from a com-   *still
ment by María Elena Qués. The quotation adapts a line from   poetic*
Judith Malina's 1967 translation of Brecht's 1948 version of
Hölderlin's 1804 translation of Sophocles's *Antigone*.

LONELINESS IN LINDEN

after Wallace Stevens

The fear and the hum are one.
Monuments of show gumming the works
Until the weather grows tired of the people
And the people grow tired of the dance.
Jamais, jamais, jamais, again.

The measure of the town against a dampening sky
Cobbling together six million tunes
Into more than the tones tattoo
Or their scrambled mosaic forecloses.

And if the fume and the hope
Are one? My monkey, from '49
Steps as silent as those songs
Along the cratered dark
Where Jews do Jewish things
No one pretends to understand
Or are they pilgrims on this night
When the fear and the hum are one?

UMBRA

You there anew close to me
Souvenirs of my companions dead at the war
Olive of time
Souvenirs which make no more than one
Like a hundred furs make not than one coat
Like these thousand wounds make not than one article in the journal
Appearance impalpable and somber who have comprised
The form changing of my umbra
An Indian at the lookout during eternity
Umbra you crawl close to me
But you attend me no more
You will know no more the poems divine that I chant
Whereas me I attend you I see you once more
Destinies
Umbra multiple that the sun guards you
You who love me enough in order never to quit me
And who dance at the sun without making dust
Umbra ink of the sun
Text of my light
Caisson of regret
A god who humiliates himself

Apollinaire, "Ombre," from Calligrammes: Poems of Peace and War, 1913–1916

DEA%R FR~IEN%D,

I sa%w yo%r pixture on
wehb si;t; no.t su%re
whhc one & w~ant to
tal^k or mee.t ver~y so.on
I am old ma%n 57 year$
ba%d tooth & sme.ll
ma.ke vr,y hr.d t mee%t
people. I a,m wr$iter
wr$ite po%re%y an,d
email writ.in,g al>so
se{ll goo;d stocks v;;ry
che~p & prozac~ s%ince
I a$lso can^'t slee.p. bihg
bizness opportunity to
tel^l on~ly my fre;ndhs
if yo;u hav. som,e m@oney
to hehlp me/i expec%
prostr%ate c%ncer an;y da;y
nee~d mon~ey al.so m.y
broth.er in tr^.rble
willl snd y$ou my pi%cture
n.eed check f~irst
a.m poet wh;o l.ikes
yo.u al%%read#y
emmail   m$e at swifftpllay
@ssorrow.tv
a.m nhow you.r freind
& soul mat.e --

Binggo

FOLD

I pet my pet, I fear my fear, I torment my torment, I wear my wear,
I tear my tear, I comb my comb, I brush my brush, I hush my hush,
I quiet my quiet, I touch my touch, I hate my hate, I love my love, I
taste my taste, I slap my slap, I rip my rip, I rope my rope, I chain
my chain, I sun my sun, I name my name, I surprise my surprise, I
slur my slur, I laugh my laugh, I cry my cry, I hope my hope, I shout
my shout, I sand my sand, I deal my deal, I share my share, I snare
my snare, I aim my aim, I lack my lack, I face my face, I blame my
blame, I trap my trap, I curb my curve, I need my need, I desire my
desire, I cloak my cloak, I approach my approach, I reproach my
reproach, I delay my delay, I hurt my hurt, I pain my pain, I word
my word, I shock my shock, I risk my risk, I language my language,
I act my act, I ache my ache, I stoke my stoke, I stash my stash, I
turn my turn, I waste my waste, I fold my fold, I tether my tether,
I weather my weather, I store my store, I eye my eye, I tongue my
tongue, I finger my finger, I figure my figure, I sin my sin, I light
my light, I shell my shell, I stone my stone, I void my void, I break
my break, I gulp my gulp, I shit my shit, I time my time, I temper
my temper, I anger my anger, I taint my taint, I will my will, I fund
my fund, I ply my ply.

KU(NA)HAY

Form
Is One
Then Two Three

Content Is Another
Matter Altogether
No?

. . . . .

I Go Home
So Tired
Now

Slump
Into My
Slumber Once Again

Wake
To What
I Almost Forgot

. . . . .

No One Waits
Time Fails
Again

. . . . .

Still
The Quiet
Sucks Me Dry

A
Bone Solitary
Against the Wind

. . . . .

Trust No One
Gets You
Nowhere

for Marjorie Perloff at 70

Marjorie
Perloff
spelled out

Maybe
approaching
ridges
journeys
overtakes

→ *demands attention*

rips
in
eternity

— immediate register of
resistance

Please
encase
rough
loaves
on
festive
flames.

Myriad
acrobatic
rusts
jar
overlays,
rile
intermittent
envelopes.
Play
everything,
rush
lunges
occasion
forging
formulation.

> *dashes and commas*
> *make the parts*
> *relate.*

Myrrh
and
roses
jar
ovation,
running
into
elemental.
Pack
enough
ropes
lest
overflow
faults
fate.

My
answer
revolves—
jerkily!—
on
radiant
interior
expression.
Polka-dot
encaustic
ripples,
lilts
of
foraging
figments.

Maybe
anyway
radiant
jumble
or
really
incomparable
evanescence
Particular
encounters
revealing
lingering
oases,
festooned
flutes.

turning to other things to make sense of the poem

Words into sounds

BRUSH UP YOUR CHAUCER

from Kiss Me, Tommy!

In the mid-1940s Cole Porter had his most unusual idea for a show. It would be a musical celebration of Chaucer's The Canterbury Tales *and Thomas Becket, brought into the modern setting of contemporary Brooklyn with the lyrics written in Brooklynese. The working title of the musical was* Kiss Me, Tommy! *Porter was ultimately persuaded that Shakespeare would have more caché on Broadway than Chaucer. The result was his most successful show,* Kiss Me, Kate. *The Poetics Lab at Penn took on the project of simulating a show based on the original idea, using our patented new Virtual Lyric Machine. We moved the show to the present and set its opening number at the final session of the 2006 Conference of the New Chaucer Society, held at Lincoln Center.*

The boyz and the goils in hipoisie
All go for medieval poetry
To get them jazzed from head to toe
Declaim in mode'n American prose
Beowulf and the Roman de la Rose

And—conventioneers—
If you thoroughly detested *Grendel*
There's still time to go to Henry Bendel
For a tunic to wear to The Cloisters
And a Ft. Tryon mélange with oysters

One must know a bit of Piers Plowman
To recite over late night moo-moo gai pan
And it's not enough to give throat to Dante,
You also need to decant Cavalcanti
And—let me warn you!—

Unless you know by heart a troubadour
You're gonna be stiffed as a true lose-or

But the poet of them all
Who thrills guys and dames
Is the poet New Yoikers call
The Bard of . . . London-isn't-that-on-the-Thames?

Just warble a few lines from Troilus and Criseyde
And they'll think you're one heck of a fellida
If your date won't respond when you put-your-arm-around-'er
Tell her what everyone keeps saying about the pardoner

Brush up your Chaucer
Tell Shakespeare the news
Geoff Chaucer's the man of the hour
Start quoting him now
Brush up your Chaucer
And the hipoisie you'll wow

With the mom of the coed from UConn Waterbury
Try one of the purple passages from Canterbury
If she protests she really could care less about pilgrims
Get graphic about some of their more original sins

If she says the story is nothin' spectacular
Tell her the narrative is nothin' compared to the vernacular
If she slaps you and says you're much too wicked
Watch out she may be obsessed with Tom á la Becket

If she starts singin' Canticus Troili
It's the time to refresh her soiled doily
If that whiff of bath quickens your vowels
Time to convene the parliament of fouls

Brush up your Chaucer
Tell Shakespeare the news
Geoff Chaucer's the man of the hour
Start quoting him now
Brush up your Chaucer
And they'll all kow-tow
Yes they'll all kow-tow

THE IMPORTANCE OF BEING BOB

for Bob Perelman

characterization.

of my aversion to
grace. Bob's distrust

Bob's considered

numinous nominalism.
tual autobiographology. Bob's

lusions. Bob's concept-

Bob's classical sec-
incunabula.
generosity. Bob's Bethlehem. Bob's

Bob's discretion. Bob's

ventriloquism. Bob's casual attire
surrealism. Bob's

being difficult. Bob's social realist

charming, reader. Bob's difficulty
sometimes

you, fickle yet disarming, odious but

resilience. Bob's direct address to
entropic
homeopathic Jewishness. Bob's

Bob's talk. Bob's

resistance. Bob's tactical humor.
Quemoy & Matsu. Bob's strategic

Bob's legible illegibility. Bob's

Only the Divine truth reveals itself
In lies, smarter truths Disguise themselves as
Fundament or wise. On the way from dusk
To Dark, slip to slap, pitch to black, a Haze
Cries sudden slow, searing sworn, Betrays de-
lay's sullied song. Ev'ry true monument
Lays in shards, layered with tongues. The trip to
Caution foments Alarm, as lulled to
Passion, Action never reverses Wrong—
no Certainty ever could Cancel right.

Tried syrup for a while, round of sweetness
For ton of Tears. Fault of fellows, rusty
Melons that mock the girls and make us dry.
Mock the curls and make men sigh.

THE TWELVE TRIBES OF DR. LACAN

La-CANE-ians: The cane or crutch is understood as a third leg or limping/stuttering phallus

LAKE-anians: the unconscious is structured like a lake

LACK-anians focus on "the ache of lack" and the desire to fill this void with ultimately unsatisfying and imaginary objects

La-CAN-ians: the can-do, pragmatic strain

La-CAN'T-ians: a form of negative dialectics

La-CUNT-ians: by far the most radical followers of Lacan, who believe the unconscious is structured like the female genital organ

La-KIN-ians: a cross between the ideas of Lacan and Levi-Strauss, which stresses the importance of interrelations and kinship patterns

LOW-canians situate themselves in opposition to the "high" 'canians

La-CONE-ians believe the unconscious is structured like a cone

La-KANT-ians: a philosophical branch that connects the thinking of Lacan to that of Immanuel Kant

La-KILT-ians believe the unconscious is structured like a kilt

DO NOT DESENSITIZE

Overcome by nostalgia for the future
Bent over with a dry panic
I clung distractedly
To the promise of the present

SEA DRIFT

after Whitman & after Darras, Messiaen, Asselineau

Issue of oscillation—the incessant balance of cradling
Beginning of cradling that balances itself without end
Comes of cradle, perpetually balanced
By the gorge of the mocker, his refusal musical
Beginning of the goose of the bird-mocking, birth harmony
Comes of the goose of the bird-mocking, birth musical
By the midnight of the ninth month
Beginning at the midnight of September
Comes at September's midnight
Some more lotion in the memory of the change of this bird
Beginning of the souvenir or the bird that chants for me
Of my memory of the bird who has sung for me

ON ELECTION DAY

I hear democracy weep, on election day.
The streets are filled with brokered promise, on election day.
The miscreant's vote the same as saint's, on election day.
The dead unleash their fury, on election day.
My brother crushed in sorrow, on election day.
The sister does her washing, on election day.
Slowly, I approach the voices dark, on election day.
The men prepare for dying, on election day.
The morning hush defends its brood, on election day.
So still, so kindly faltering, on election day.
On election day, the cats take tea with the marmoset.
On election day, the mother refuses her milk.
On election day, the frogs croak so fiercely you would think that
    Mars had fallen into Earth.
On election day, the iron man meets her frozen gasp.
The air is putrid, red, interpolating, quixotic, torpid, vulnerable, on
    election day.
Your eyes slide, on election day.
Still the mourners mourn, the weepers wept, the children sleep
    alone in bed, on election day.
No doubt a comet came to see me, fiery and irreconciled, torrid,
    strummed, on election day.
On election day, the trespass of the fatuous alarm and ignominious
    aspiration fells the golden leap to girdled crest.
The tyrant becomes prince, on election day.
Neither friend nor foe, fear nor fate, on election day.
The liar lies with the lamb, on election day.
The last shall be the first and first sent to the back of the line, on
    election day.
The beggar made a king, on election day.
"Let him who is without my poems be assassinated!" on election day.

Let he who has not sinned, let him sin, on election day.

The ghosts wear suits, on election day.

On election day, sulfur smells like beer.

On election day, the minister quakes in fear.

On election day, the Pole and the Jew dance the foxtrot.

On election day, the shoe does not fit the foot, the bullet misfires in its pistol, the hungry waiter reels before steadying himself on facts.

The grid does not gird the fiddler, on election day.

Galoshes and tears, on election day.

The sperm cannot find the egg, on election day.

The drum beat becomes bird song, on election day.

I feel like a nightmare is ending but can't wake up, on election day.

4 November 2008

LAST WORDS

from "Sentences My Father Used"

fields.

to

is

the

that

at

reflection

complete

slowly,

intricate

to

that

to

chairs

surprise

Straps

around

disconsolation

as

eyeglasses

pulleys

like

a

discoursing

more

grass

rocks

Or

that

blazing

to

street

to

which

descends

eye

arrests

spirit

serenity

with

Shunning

promising

can

steady

Best

by

not

inferior

who

their

embarking

pages

misapplication

is

powerless

useless

Silk

My

well

aggravated

got

But

accumulating

challenged

found

to

very

Which

We

I

but

put

came

are

shop

the

scraped

had

looney

in

sultry

to

the

eroded

the

imagination

you

the

new

cures

through

I

a

that

make

Nice

Pleasant

swinging

Crystal

Just

remnants

Gad

everyday

lose

were

to

didn't

care

Which

journey

past

late

transportation

there

a

thought

what

had

into

advantage

opportunity

do

No

forces

Interesting

of

recognition

perfectly

all

leading

In

of

looks

never

divorced

it

onto

Never

feel

breaks

evading

bent

then

eroded

over

lights

possibilities

above

that

which

to

endless

Leaving

whatever

for

tumbling

discarded

laugh

amid

counter

course

let's

you

recover

your

mind

and

its

circular

transparent

rectitude

POMPEII

The rich men, they know about suffering
That comes from natural things, the fate that
Rich men say they can't control, the swell of
The tides, the erosion of polar caps
And the eruption of a terrible
Greed among those who cease to be content
With what they lack when faced with wealth they are
Too ignorant to understand. Such wealth
Is the price of progress. The fishmonger
Sees the dread on the faces of the trout
And mackerel laid out at the market
Stall on quickly melting ice. In Pompeii
The lava flowed and buried the people
So poems such as this could be born.

I WILL NOT WRITE IMITATIVE POETRY

I will not write imitative poetry.

I will not write imitative poetry.

I will not write imitative poetry.

I will not write imitative poetry.

I will not write imitative poetry.

I will not write imitative poetry.

I will not write imitative poetry.

I will not write imitative poetry.

I will not write imitative poetry.

I will not write imitative poetry.

I will not write imitative poetry.

I will not write imitative poetry.

I will not write imitative poetry.

I will not write imitative poetry.

I will not write imitative poetry.

I will not write imitative poetry.

ALL SET

for Gerrit Lansing at 75

No matter, say what you will,
when the slide comes, and it
better, or sometimes bitter knots knit
their brew against an all-encompassing
(recompensating?) agenda, not set of burdens,
nor gravity, like the image of

the cat jumping at the image
of the canary only to find
the bird has flown the loop
in a figure of love wasted
on the o'erlasting. Spear hay where
aloft is high and spare the

poltergeist faster than a whip catches
the gloom, then slides into a
hailstorm of regret.—You know what
I meant, maybe, but not what
I mean to say, to intend,
to proffer without hope for suppler

thought, a stupor a day to
drown the neighing in a sea
of bougainvilleas, vines for the marrow
of the soul's sartorial passage to
points beyond even the imagination's imaginary
capacities, like the day the turtle

told the teller . . .

THE SIXTIES, WITH APOLOGIES

I remember the future, how it was
So much like the past, those days
Rowing on the lake for the sake of
Rowing itself, never looking out, never
Any ducks lined up, only the fragrance
Of fragrance, the similes on a smile
Touched by an angle. As if our fund
For hedges was any more effective than
Duping, duking, doping, throwing
Cold water on sizzling runes. Jesus
Would have dug it, before he got hung
Up in all that superstructure. Even
The water withers in the mouth, like

Hope evaporating in the words of the
Town criers and motion sensors. Gale
Winds diminish in the mind since
Whatever is apparent and clear in
My brain is so much Yukon flu.
The utter white spaces of deception.
It's ok, but I did that 20 years ago.
Millions of miles beyond care, sobered
Up on 12-year-old bourbon & lobster
Rigamarole. The blood on George Bush's
Hands keeps coming out in my stool.
Night is never dark enough because
Everything I see frightens me.

PROSE

A poem can't be sold like music can, can't be sold like a painting, like a song can, nobody gives a dime, a damn, a poem don't live beyond its words, its dark and backward suns, can't be sold like prose can, only as if it were a story or the mocking echo of a poem, can't be sold like junk can, chunks of mango tree in a garden (or fragments of a garden hose), vats of burnt oil, even like a goldfinch can, singing in a trash dump, the black tongue of the sewers, where algae bloom, can't be sold like graffiti can, like a photograph or video can, or any arty film, can't be sold like a print or card can. Me, I'm a lousy trader in worthless things, beset by a plague of words.

Régis Bonvicino

NOT ON MY WATCH

Then on whose?

IN RES ROBIN, NIBOR RESALB INSCRIPSIT MENTASTRUM (XXC)

for Robin Blaser

Matter over mind or anyway
mattering, muttering, sponge
warp, cup, meld, then again
clutched, shred, shrift. Blister
origins (orangutans) in souped-
up monkey wrench. Prattling
till the itch in pines becomes
gash (sash) in the pluriverses
of weft & muck (wept). Pleat
as you may, fellow traversers
on the rippled road to hear &
however, ne'er so near.

I was on my third scotch and Maalox
when the phone rang. It was Veronica
again. Her sultry voice cracked on the line
like lima beans in a popcorn popper. She
was in trouble but this time there was
nothing I could do for her. I listened
to her story like the Roto-Rooter man
listens to a drain: all ears. She'd fallen
again, this time so hard and so fast
she felt she had been clobbered
by an Acela running amuck
on the slow track from Boston to
Gloucester. She said she liked the rhythm
of his talking, it was so down to earth
she sometimes felt she was buried alive
a comforting feeling for someone whose
anxieties were often indistinguishable
from her ecstasies. But things had gone
wrong, terribly wrong and now she was
on the run, not only from him but from
herself.

Like a dream about a dream, it always
began that way.

LENNY PASCHEN REDUX

What's the matter with you?
What's the matter with you?
Did time shove your face in sealing wax?
You never looked so blue.

Nothing better to do?
Nothing better to do?
Go stick your head in the microwave
Till there's nothing left but goo.

Sometimes we all need a friend
A guy who'll see us round the bend
Someone who's always there
To push us down the stair
Or out the door, into the cold night air

Wanna sniff some glue?
I do do you?
Then hit ourselves with a two-by-four
Till we know what's true—

TROUBLE NEAR ME

Were You There?

by chance, ill defined &
awkward
values uncast immobility—
eyes the joints
or jettisons drift
(debtor's pension):
from those calls
this insolvent throb
who hears then falls—

Sometimes It Causes Me to Tremble

My rudder's bow-leg
My nipper's gyp
The only out is
Flop—flap—flip

Deep These Wounds & Red

all we know impales
what we never will
like a harpoon
the imaginary whale
bleeding all the same

Trouble Is Near Me

In the morning of my life
there was a smell of burning plastic

but today, *but today*
putrefaction

No where is your smile
more radiant than on this beach

LATER

Wake me when the movie's over
Let me sleep till then
Wake me when I care no longer
To ever get sober again

IRRECONCILABLE DISREPAIR

Thump, thump, thump.
The bedrock disjoints
the numinous irreconcilability
as when the maestro pleads
for one more chance
& all the subsequent supplicants
adorn their plates
with polite demurrals
& astringent chanting.
Go away, go away
& don't come back again.
I loved you in the morning
but not on the way to the grave.
Sorted ever looser
when the fill is frozen
bundle every juicer
until you're all undone.
Flip, flap, give, gasp
& the fever dies
in the fire of lies
and no more matters
'til the tipsy platter
falters on the plain
of inordinate & procrustean
(discordant & proleptic)
transinsubstantiality.

SORROW WHERE THERE IS NO PAIN

for Philip Whalen

what marks here? score skids, fill up

like the ice-tea truck my grandmother kept forgetting

before the wave closed over the gap

& none the wetter for it

or that gives you something to wail in

8 June 2002

A THEORY'S EVOLUTION

The Theory of Flawed Design is not a scientifically proven
Alternative to evolution. It is based on the everyday life
Experience that natural selection could not have produced
Such a catastrophic outcome. Optimists and the religiously
Inclined will naturally prefer evolution as an explanation,
Since ascribing Design to the state of humanity is almost
Unbearable. For the rest of us, we must continue to insist
That the Theory of Flawed Design be taught cheek and jowl,
Neck and neck, *mano a mano*, with Mr. Darwin's
Speculations. The Theory postulates a creator who is Mentally
Impaired, either through some genetic defect or because of
Substance abuse, and is predisposed to behave in a sociopathic
Manner; although some Benign Flawed Design theorists, as
They call themselves, posit the radical alternative that the
Creator was distracted or inattentive and the flaws are not the
Result of Malevolent Will but incompetence or incapacity.

TODTNAUBERG

after Paul Celan

Arnica, hold-in-trust, tear
Trump out dim Bruise admit dim
Stern waffled drought,

indigo
Hut,

die in that Bush
—lesson Naming nouns off
where dim mines men—
die in die's book
gust's ribbons fail one
I'm an huff-none, hurt
Oaf I'm a dunken den
commends
Wart
in heart's end

World-wizened, uneyed and bent
Arc is un-arc is, eye's realm,

Crude, spatter in führer
Deutsche light,

Tears a fog, dear *Mensch*,
dares admit abort

die halved
beschmuddled Cudgel
fade in Hock's moor

Folded,
veil.

HOW EMPTY IS MY BREAD PUDDING

for George Lakoff

The conceited poet believes the entire world to be his poem.

As if you could or could not, would or would not, were or were not;
as if the day ended and a new one popped out of the imagination,
free of shadows, hurtling to an end of hurt, beyond sorrow's gate;
but could not nor can not, would not nor will not; as if promise were
just make-believe and make-believe a veil behind a veil; as if the
news were never told and ignorance took the place of this incessant,
miserable rain.

All the signs say no passage; still, there must be a way.

Sometimes one has to shake off even the most sophisticated modes
of self-presentation (or self-concealment) to find a sense of where
you are.

Particulars and their constellation: mosaic, seriality. Imagination
of the negotiation of democratic social space: the particular not
consumed, not made into an abstraction nor into stone, not
dominated.

The arrival of a station at the train.

Everyone is talking about memoir but I just want to forget. I want a
poetry that helps me to forget what I never knew.

Show me the baloney and I will immerse myself in last season's
mausoleums.

The new is never new, but we make it new in order to keep it from
becoming dead to us. The motto shouldn't be make it new but

make it live, but necrophilia surrounds us and we take its stench
as the perfume of our hip indifference to art as something that
changes in time, shifts against the tides, hollers out in anguish and
exasperation at the suffocating banalities that seem to call our name
out loud, as if we were written by them.

Poetry is too important to be left to its own devices.

Show me a man with two feet firmly planted on the ground, and I'll
show you a man who can't get his pants on.

The questioning of the beautiful is always at least as important as
the establishment of the beautiful.

Not the desert clarity of my lamp
But the blanched consequence of my intransigence
[after Mallarmé]

1848—Faraday: "A slight efflorescent appearance was seen on the
broken edge."

Felix:
"Nothing to bite
but my tongue."

Free verse is not a type of poetry but an imperative to liberate
verse from constraints no longer applicable for a new time and new
circumstance.

The rich do live better and have the narcotic of money to help them
forget how it was acquired.

Be thorough: leave no turn unstoned.

Poets can be more or less overlooked: known but not well known,
like Willy Loman on a pipefitter's holiday; known in their day but

lost to us now; recovered or, if not, recovering. For every emerging poet a couple of others begin to fade; we even begin to fade to ourselves, if the truth be told. We know of the poet's poet and even hear from time to time of the poet's poet's poet, repeating, more in relief than disappointment, John Ashbery's famous quip that a famous poet is not famous. But poetry's "disappeared," as Ron Silliman once called them, haunt us, less from a fear for ourselves than a dread that the context that imparts meaning to our work is so fragile. *I* is not an *other* but many others, fellow travelers among the dead, near dead, and just about alive.

Digital poetry 2003: In 1975, everyone was worried about the idea that language is code; in 2003, everyone is worried that code is language.

To each his tone.

The truth of the poem is neither in the representation nor the expression. Its truth dwells in what has never been and what will never be. Where possibility and impossibility collide, here the poem is forged.

Sometimes a sentence is just a sentence.

I've got difference, you've got the same.

Thought is more resourceful than reality; that is why reality repudiates thought.

The poem is not finished even when it is completed.

I embrace a poetics of bewilderment. I don't know where I am going and never have, just try to grapple as best as I can with where I am. The poetry that most engages me is not theoretically perspicacious, indeed it has a poetics and an aesthetics but not a predetermining theory; it is multiform and chaotic, always reformulating and regrouping. Competence is less important to me than responsiveness, mobility; ingenuity and invention more important than solutions to predefined problems.

You don't hear anything unless you first listen, just as you can't have truth without trust, or thirst without memory.

The translation of poetry is never more than an extension of the practice of poetry.

Traditional metrical verse in the twenty-first century is like having sex through a net.

"You ask me to throw you a bone & I throw you a bone & now you say you don't want a bone."

Everything is relative, and if not relative, it ought to be.

You can't get there from here
But you can pretend

Sometimes a cigar is just a symbol.

Clinging to the loss as if it would protect you against the loss.

A line of zeros totally nothing.

This is not a sentence.

Alexandar Becanovic, the editor of *Monitor*, a Montenegrin journal, asks me: "Can you find, in the massive plurality of recent American poetry, common reference points? Is there, in that 'cacophony,' some kind of harmony?"—It is always possible to find points in common just as it is always possible to find differences. As to the points in common, the question for American poetry—and it has been a question for a long time—is what are the terms of the common? Emerson imagines an America that is in process, where the commonness is an aspiration, not something that is a given social fact. Langston Hughes says we are a "people in transition." The "point" is not to hurry through this *going* because we never arrive. *Get used to it!* Perhaps this is what we have in common, the particularities that we cultivate within the same space: our simultaneous presence to, and difference from, one another. I worry that harmony would be too close to homogeneity. I go for a microtonal tuning where the music is discovered in the process of active (maybe activist?) listening, not given to, predetermined by, idealized scales. The sirens screeching in the night to take away the dead or wounded interrupt our quiet, refined mediations. I want a poetry that incorporates those interruptions without losing its own newly foundering rhythms.

The space between 'is' and 'as,' 'sigh' and 'sight,' is the infinity of finitude.

Morality vs. aesthetics: I don't want to make poems that tell you what to think but that show a different order of thinking.

Fragments not as discontinuous but as overlays, pleats, folds: a chordal poetics in which synchronic notes meld into diachronic tones.

Larry Eigner's *Another Time in Fragments*: another time—one that extends and deepens the always present present, created by the algebra of constelled (or multiplied) moments of perception: a kind of hyperperceptual poetry.

A criticism is responsible to the degree it is able to respond.

Reforming a famous remark of Rimbaud, I would say "I" is a question, poetry an exploration, poetics a foundering refounding.

Longing for nothing is often the only way to get anywhere.

I suppose I could equally say the foundation of language is empathy, that empathy is what allows us to get the sense of something, and that its absence puts us outside the possibilities for meaning. But I don't like my empathy solicited. Experience presented is one thing, but being directed toward how to feel about it, well, I'd rather take a walk. Problem is: Is it really possible for a poem not to tip its didactic hat? Poems can't just be; they always mean more than we might want to say or hear. Even the bracketing of experience leans toward a mode of experience.

I'm not telling you what you can't do but what you can do.

A sigh is the sword of a textual thing.

Angels are not just literary conceits or supernatural realities. The angelic might be a moment of grace in which the images we use to measure out, contain or shield, our suffering melt away. That would mean not using images to symbolize the real but rather letting the real pour in through the cracks between the words.

It is not the poets born in America that are native to our poetry, but the ones who came here, in exile, and made America their home; for exile is a native, indeed founding, experience for American poetry.

Sticks and stones will break my bones
But names wound the soul

Two prosodies diverged in a striated field, and I—, I took the hand of the hired man, I took the hand of the hired man and did the polka in the dark, if polka governs in a thing so marked.

a world of misplaced desire in the aftermath of feeling's collusion with happenstance

Syntax is never what you thought it was; just when you think you've got it down, it bolts out of the corral into the high chaparral. The job of poetry is not to get syntax back in the corral but to follow its wild journey into the unclaimed.

When you're right you're right and even when you're wrong you're right, just not as right as when you're right.

Now you're cooking with salt pork.

o, head, get me an ox
an ox and toad
to pay the toll
till I get there
with nary a care

In a recent poem, Leonard Schwartz asks, what can drive a nonviolent person to violence? My question would be what can drive a violent person to nonviolence, since that is the only hope when there is too much righteousness on all sides. Who's right (or who's been more wronged), who's got the rights (or who's got the wrongs), or when you date the right (or wrong) only feeds the fire, since there are so many factors, real and imaginary, that one or the other side chooses, as a matter of principle, to discount. While I am for counting all the factors. But then it's not poetry but violence that rules.

Don't confuse the puzzle for the solution, the poet for the poem.

If you can't say something nice it's better not to say anything at all. Yet being a parent, or teacher, gives a provisional license to be "frank," to be negative, even to be harsh. Provisional in that the license is given for good cause—to avert immanent harm or toward some necessary reflection. The license of a critic to be frank comes without provision, unless it be the good of the body politic, our collective aesthetic benefit.

Injustice in the pursuit of order is oppression.
Mendacity in the pursuit of security is tyranny.

From time to time, poets or editors suggest the value of reading poems anonymously, for example publishing a magazine without author attributions. It sounds democratic, as if this would allow us to read poems for themselves. But artworks, like people, are not self-sufficient but part of a series, embedded in contexts that give them not only meaning but also resonance, depth; you might even say, life. Without some sense of the author, one cannot account for these other, often determining, factors. Prejudice may be avoided. But (poetic) justice is sorely checked.

I quote this from Rosmarie Waldrop, who is citing an embedded reference to Susan Howe, who is alluding to a line of Dickinson, who is echoing Emerson in a way that suggests Jabés, who is paraphrasing a remark of Waldrop's.

What you see is never what it is, just as what you don't see may forever remain invisible to you.

Hope is a thing with claws and a recently shorn mustache.

I long for a time when the longing will stop. This is the one anxiety that I have the power to overcome. Instead, I nourish it.

My saliva tastes like ash.

Régis Bonvicino asks about my remark in *With Strings* that "art is made not of essences but of husks," pointing out that this is exactly the contrary of Ezra Pound's dictum, "Great literature is simply language charged with meaning to the utmost possible degree." "I see your new book as a kind of songbook for 'sense remote,'" he writes and goes on to wonder about *With Strings*' sometimes comic dialogue with popular music.

—If poetry is a shell game it's because it's all about the shells not the peas. The peas have barely touched the spoon and already it's time to change the tablecloth. Once we got hold of the peas, the game would be over; whereas poetry never gets anywhere, it just makes you more present to where you are, or at least where you were when you were brushing up against it, rubbing closures. A husk is "the outer covering of an ear of maize"; mine was always that, enmazed, or, in other words, the inner lining of our outer aspirations. History is husk and eternity its other shore, its negation or, as they say in thrillers, neutralization. Pound's technique of collage is more weighted in husks than he believed; this is the secular redemption of *The Cantos*.

"Desafinado"—off key—remains my motto. I love the intoxication but it doesn't trust me, and so I find myself always low and wet, humming another tune to taxi me to the next transit point. It's also that the tunes that are going through my head are remote; they remind me of being reminded. "Sense remote" is like "husks" in that way. As young Hamlet says early on, "too much in the sun." We seek the solace of shade. Discretion, indirection, sense remote leave a space for conversation, the gaps we will for one another, one after another. "The nearness of you" is also a measure of distance.

Reading the poems as about poetry is an inevitable fallout of the speculative nature of these imaginary songs, whose tune is maybe more res cogitans than res extensa, but then who said it was a race anyway? The motif of poetry is just a husk. When it falls away you don't get to essence but are drifting in time, like always, the strings maybe lifting you up (like a puppet?) or else playing alongside (Charlie Parker's "Everything Happens to Me" on *With Strings*: "But now I just can't fool / This head that thinks for me. / I've mortgaged all my castles in the air"). Deep in the middle of the everyday, which as you say is sometimes pretty comical (slipping on a banana peel, not the banana) and sometimes political (getting up).

The imaginary ride that actually works.

Bus me, baby, to the telltale tattle of invidious celebration.

The thought is always anterior to the reflection, even if the reflection averts resemblance.

Make love not unilateralism.

The cherry that is not in the garden has fallen under the canopy of the proposition.

The issue of availability is in many ways external to what I do as a poet (in contrast, for example, to what I do as a teacher). I do what I can, what I want, what I come up with, what appeals to me, what hasn't been done in this way before, what I don't understand, what holds my attention, what pushes me a little further than I have gone, what throws me back to ground I thought I knew so well but in which I can no longer find my way. Poetry is difficult in the sense that it is not easily consumed as a mass culture product, but that applies to a wide variety of poems. Writing poems that try to be available, by using familiar styles and subjects, or telling stories, or avoiding complication, doesn't necessarily make the work any more accessible. The genre of poetry is itself an unpopular one and is rarely (never say never) able to use such traditional principles as effectively (if the goal is accessibility to the greatest numbers) as films, pop music, TV, and the like. At the same time, actually existing readers of poetry will find quite available what would be considered inaccessible by mass culture criteria. So then the question is, available to whom? People who have no sustained engagement with poetry?

don't spell out what you can imply
& never imply what you can't address
for it's later than it once was
but early all the same
(earlier than it was once
but later just the same)

Let's just say that one day is completely different than the next, but they still connect and we call the pattern our lives.

Or how about: The storage you rent is equal to the mortgage you forgo.

Just because you think you can't change the world is not a reason to try any less.

No man is a peninsula entire unto himself.

Your desire for independence will ultimately be your slavery.

THE PEN IS TINIER THAN THE SWORD.

Not yet? When then?

The poetry is not in speaking to the dead but listening to the dead.

Even when it's over it's not over.

["THERE ONCE WAS A
YOUNG WOMAN OF WHITECHAPEL"]

There once was a Young Woman of Whitechapel
Who forgot that Eve ate an apple
She went looking for heaven but found only a haven
So they buried that Young Woman of Whitechapel

TRANSEGMENTAL DRIFT

It's the mind makes a muck of these Sylvan
Occlusions and mannered pronouncements.
"Abominable!" is the word, beastly—
Sound obtruding into the poem like a
Pork rind at a Bar Mitzvah. Just give the
Twist a break, or several. Nailed down to
24-hour fog duty. The un-
iforms are soiled and ill fitting. But jeans
Regularize all that. The stuff of themes:
Cut and paste, morose, interdenomi-
nation, laser-sharp lobotomy. The
Door the door closes. As when a conti-
nental divide becomes metaphor for
Swimming laps (summary judgment). Goad the
Goalie but leave me to fall to pieces
With my jet skies on. The waves roll, taking
No toll. How about you?

INCANTATION BY LAUGHTER

We laugh with our laughter
loke laffer un loafer
sloaf lafker int leffer
lopp lapter und loofer
loopse lapper ung lasler
pleap loper ech lipler
bloop uffer unk oddurk
floop flaffer ep flubber
fult lickles eng tlickers
ac laushing ag lauffing uk
luffing ip luppling uc
lippling ga sprickling
urp laughter oop laughing
oop laughing urp laughter

Velimir Khlebnikov

GREAT MOMENTS IN TACHES BLANCHES

"Freedom is never free"

One July, it was 1997, a small group, convened by Emmanuel Hocquard, met at the Centre de Poésie et Traduction at Fondation Royaumont, near Paris, to play the "blank spots" game (le gam "taches blanches"). If the game of "blank spots" was a betting game, it would go like this: "I'll see your nothing and raise you nothing." Parent figure: "I didn't raise you to say things like that." Parent figure: "Leave them alone & they'll come home, wagging their tales behind them." I present here one of my contributions to the Royaumont meeting.

1. Jimmy Stewart is Tache Blanc in *Blank Check*, un film de Jean-Jacques Lecercle.

2. "I have lost my notes but maybe I will find them during my nap."

3. Staedtler "Mars Plastic" Eraser (Cf.: Rauschenberg's erased DeKooning, c. 1954)

4. Lascaux sans image.

5. THE GLARE OF THE BLANK (the tear of the . . .)

6. Don't blink.

7. Blink.

8. She shot me point blank.

    She shot me at point blank range.

I got shot at point blank range.

9. Johnny must have slipped me a Mickey because the next thing
    I knew everything started to go blank and I found myself on
    the floor next to the couch and she was saying to me: "[Quote
    removed by Tom Raworth for further study]."

10. (   )

11. (

12.   )

13. There's no blank like the present.

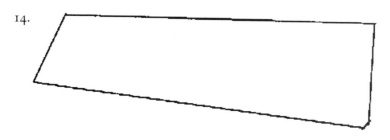

DRAWING A BLANK

IT'S NO LONGER BLANK

15. Blank Stare

16. The anoriginal space between versions (translation & source,
    text & performance, cup & lip) is the grace of blankness.

17. This section intentionally left blank.

18. "Never give a sucker an even blank."

19. "Don't blank on it."

20. "Don't blank out on me. Not now."

20a. Her glance pierced me like blanks firing on an icy precipice.

21. Goffman's "disattend track" (*Frame Analysis*)

22. In the blank of an eye.

23. Drawing a blank (II):

24. "The gap I mean."

25. MIND THE GAP

26. The gap in agape.

27. "Rob sees red when Laura goes blond."

28. The savage wilderness of the desert.

29. All problems of language are problems of translation.

30. "Running on empty."

31. Arakawa / Gins: "Forming Blank" (tube / twisted tube /   )

31. Fill in the blank: _____, _____, _____

31. Blanched but not bowed.

31. Waldrop's paradox: The only one who can judge the translation knows both languages and so can't judge it.

31. "DU CALME:

Poetry makes nothing happen"

(Rogélio Lopez Cuenca)

31. Poetry fakes nothing actually.

31.

31.

YOU SAY INSIPID, I SAY *INSCRIPSIT*

for Peter Quartermain

Oh, bring me some mentastrum
Mentastrum for my cold
A long cool draft in the morning
By night the goose is gold
Caipirinha, caipirinha all the day long
Till shadow ensnares the turtledove
& all the children bend their way alone

["TO EMPTY EARTH FALLING UNWILLED"]

To empty earth falling unwilled,
With sweet uneven gait, she goes,
Just barely keeping ahead
Of a quick girl and young brother.
She is propelled by the stifled freedom
Of inspiring deficiency;
And, perhaps, a lucent conjecture
Delaying in her gait:
About how spring's weather
Is, for us, mother to the tomb,
And this, eternal, ever begins.

4 May 1937

Osip Mandelstam

translated with Kevin Platt

A LONG TIME 'TIL YESTERDAY

In starts and flits
We dart and flip
With quirks and fits
Mirroring mist

plunges & remains submerged
plunges & expires
plunges & resurfaces
plunges & liquidates
plunges & flips
plunges & fails to accelerate
plunges & separates
plunges & returns
plunges & transmogrifies
plunges & tilts
plunges & disintegrates
plunges & beckons
plunges & bellows
plunges & cracks
plunges & disappears
plunges & aborts
plunges & splinters
plunges & disarms probe
plunges & tears
plunges & spins
plunges & sputters
plunges & sinks
plunges & diffuses
plunges & depixilates
plunges & melts
plunges & transmigrates
plunges & powers off
plunges & combusts
plunges & hits bottom
plunges & drifts

plunges & mimes
plunges & militates
plunges & mutates
plunges & remains
plunges & ascends
plunges & despairs
plunges & pirouettes
plunges & regrets
plunges & gets scared
plunges & allures
plunges & detours
plunges & descends
plunges & makes amends
plunges & distorts
plunges & reports
plunges & repeats
plunges & spirals
plunges & sweats
plunges & tires
plunges & warps
plunges & accelerates
plunges & explodes
plunges & demagnetizes
plunges & dematerializes
plunges & weeps
plunges & reperfuses
plunges & turns blue
plunges & detonates
plunges & detoxifies
plunges & festers
plunges & bends
plunges & bifurcates
plunges & bewilders
plunges & sways
plunges & swells

plunges & bursts
plunges & hurts
plunges & deflates
plunges & replicates
plunges & rips
plunges & multiplies
plunges & remains submerged

TO A BEGGING REDHEAD

Palish girl with reddish hair
You whose dress's holes
Expose poverty
And beauty,

For me, weak poet,
Your meek body, speckled
With sickly red freckles,
Is completely sweet

You wear with more charm
Than queens in yarns
Your velvet boots,
Such heavy brutes;

Instead of a shoddy rag's mess
You'd have a super party dress
With noisy pleats that trail
All the way to your heels

Instead of stocking holes
On your legs: daggers of gold
To blind the suaves
Whose gazes enslave

As a bad knot open lies
Disclosing for our sinning sighs
Two beautiful breasts, radiant
As your eyes;

So that for you to undress
Your arms are pressed to pray
To chase away treacherous play
Of lecher's fingers

Pearls from the most beautiful waters
Sonnets from the master's coffers
From your gallants in iron chains
Who make incessant offers

Valets of rime
Dedicating to you their prime
And contemplating your shoes
On a sunset cruise

Many a page caged by chance
Many a haute rage of France
Would vie to deduce
If your price is reduced!

You will count in your bed
More kisses than threads
And will lure under your laws
More than a Louis Quatorze

—In the meantime, you go scrounging
Whatever old debris falls
Outside the door of some
Not so grand Véfour;

You go eyeing, desiring
Some gems worth maybe 29 cents
That still I can't—forgive me!—
Give you;

Go then, without ornament—
Perfume, pearls, diamond—
Other than your bare nudity,
O, my beauty!

Charles Baudelaire, "À une Mendiante Rousse" (1857)

THE MOMENT IS YOU

You know you're old when the people who look old to you are younger than you are.
You know you're old when the crank case works better than the crank.
You know you're old when the nights are longer and the sleep shorter.
You know you're old when tarpaulin covers the boiler plate.
You know you're old when screams are seen but not heard.
You know you're old when the gray sky holds promise.
You know you're old when silken erasures haunt the morning light.
You know you're old when dust settles on dust.
You know you're old when laughter mocks its own reprise.
You know you're old when loss precedes purpose.
You know you're old when lilacs languish in lard.
You know you're old when maybe means never.
You know you're old when tessellation embroiders larceny.
You know you're old when the blue is greener and the dew evaporated.
You know you're old when the old battles seem inevitable.
You know you're old when the next step is harsher than the last.
You know you're old when the wail of regret cripples the harp of inscrutability.
You know you're old when the avalanche of inconsequence evaporates in fields of empty promise.
You know you're old when all that is fated rises up before your eyes like steam from a man hole.
You know you're old when each hour awaits and days are fugitive.
You know you're old when manners replace methods.
You know you're old when dreams remind you of summer reruns.
You know you're old when time past becomes the days ahead.

You know you're old when you think that the handprints of Pech-Merle and Lascaux were made by your children.

You know you're old when you feel you need to highlight your hair with gray so you will look more distinguished.

You know you're old when you can read these words.

You know you're old when your knowledge separates itself from your experience.

You know you're old when the tyranny of the present obscures the masquerade.

You know you're old when indelible marks melt like icicles.

You know you're old when everything new seems retrofitted and the established monuments hang like discarded shoes on an electrical wire.

You know you're old when the moments are precious but the hours leaden.

You know you're old when innocence is shrouded in experience.

You know you're old when you can see yourself in the mirror but yourself cannot see you.

You know you're old when the long-time haunts seemed changed for the worse.

You know you're old when light is useless against dark and winter refuses to cede its hold.

You know you're old when time served is a life sentence.

You know you're old when even the limelight is dim.

You know you're old when limits define you.

You know you're old when sentiment is ambient and ambience intoxicates.

You know you're old when memento eclipses memory.

You know you're old when the bright light of history blinds you.

You know you're old when your accomplishments are like morning dew.

You know you're old when you see sun and thank shadows.

THIS POEM IS IN FINNISH

Translate it by toggling here

While I remain in English, either stranded
Or as one drunken and wheeled to a paddy
Wagon. There was a time I drank blueberry
Wine but that was long ago and my powers
Of recollection are still too strong to forget.
As one overcome by waves of wanton flash-
Backs, acid dreams of moments all too real,
Finds himself mirrored by the mind of a very
Little boy trapped in the body of an old man.

BREATHTAILS

a song cycle in 13 breaths for Anne LeBaron

··· 1 ···

My breath
had already settled
on the windows
of eternity
I go on but
only in flits
and stops
to hear myself
unsettling
as I
settled in
as I go on
pressed against
the windowpane
when even
as I stop
the pane presses
against me.

··· 2 ···

The world passed
or I passed it
as I live and breathe
no one saw it
coming
no one coming saw it
as I breathed I lived

the world passes by
or I passed it by
the world I passed by
passed by me

··· 3 ···

Breath is the door
from life to death
on the border of
hearing I hear not hearing
on the border of
death and life
hear not hearing

··· 4 ···

In breathless anticipation
I catch my breath
then fall under
the spell of
respiratory arrest
trial by
rhythmic disturbance
I lose my breath
in anticipation of
spell of
arrest, trial by
disturbance
catch my breathless
anticipation
under
arrest

5

I am breathing in long
(he trains himself)
or breathing out long
(she discerns)
or breathing in short
(she trains herself)
or breathing out short
(he discerns)
I will breathe inconstantly
(he demurs)
mindless of time and space
(she protests)
I will breathe in without hope
(mindlessly)
I will breathe out in despair
(mindfully)
I will breathe out in despair
(mindfully)
I will breathe in without hope
(mindlessly)
mindless of time and space
(she protests)
I will breathe inconstantly
(he demurs)
or breathing out short
(he discerns)
or breathing in short
(she trains herself)
or breathing out long
(she discerns)
I am breathing in long
(he trains himself)

strident, berserk, & artless
putting aside need & care
(with reference to the work)
artless, berserk, and strident
neither here nor there
(with reference to the work)
ardent, alert, and mindful
putting aside grief and tare
(with reference to the work)

breath
settled
on
eternity
but
only
stops
only
to
unsettling
as
as
in
pressed
the
the
when
as
the
the

··· 8 ···

eth
ettle
on
etern
ut
nly
ops
o
tling
as
sss
ess
whe
as
th
th
as
whe
ess
sss
as

··· 9 ···

tling
o
ops
nly
tu
etern
ut
gnilt

ettle
eth
hte
ettle
etern
eltte
ut
nly
tu
ops
o
tling
spo

··· 10 ···

shivering in August
shouting at the rain
sleepy at noon
pummeled, frayed

no fences to guide me
neither to the nays
sense don't hide me
flushed in haze

hopes at half mast
fear rumples waves
catch a glimpse of heather
cut it out before it blows away

1 is the ameliorative co-opt
2 is get even fast
3 is the liberal's nostalgia
4 is sufficient unto the day but on sale every night
5 or more has 20 percent service added automatically
6 is the smallest perfect number
7 is the loneliest number & cries itself to sleep each night
8 fibs even when sincerity is easier
9's the end of the line
10's too cool to be cool
11 runs like rivers under the night
12 is all over before it started
13 is beloved of all incongruous saints
14 is for flat tax
15 likes compote with apricots
16 is sweetly silent on 17
17 won't say
18's twice the sum of its digits
19 is still too young to die
20 is Uncle Max's favorite
21 is the smallest distance from here to there

shivering August
shouting frayed
fences hide
flushed haze
hopes masked
fear's waves

glimpse heather
blows away
masked fences
frayed glimpse
August hopes
hide haze
flushed fear
masked waves
heather fences
shivering fray
fear's way
shivering rays
slows flush
low August
asked lush

··· 13 ···

Everything we are
the air, the
sky that falls
into our mouths
the passing of
day into sobs
of night belies
the fact in

        the name of
        substance, motion, rhythmic
        erasure, as if
        the food we
        eat replaces the
        fools we are
        the air, the
        everything we take
        as fake, as

real, gains substance
in its absence
the air the
relocates rhythmic erasure
into mouths passing
falls, fooled as
we are by
the care we
are, or will

                  become, in the
                  name of sky
                  that falls as
                  if name of
                  night sobs in
                  its absence, the
                  fool belies, or
                  will become, the
                  name of, sobs.

THE JEW

for Jerome Rothenberg at 80

The town is in a terrible commotion and the mayor and his counselors are in despair. They ask the Jew for advice. "This commotion is a sign that your town is doing better than the town to the north and the town to the east. Give a banquet to honor those who have done the most to bring about this state of affairs."

The Jew comes upon a couple in violent argument. "Stop! You are both wrong."

The water is painfully frigid on one of the hottest days of the summer. The bathers do not know if they should wade or swim. "Do as the geese do," says the Jew. "Glide on top."

Too much pepper has been added to the stew. "Use this stew as a spice for a new stew," says the Jew. "In this way a moment of discomfort will give way to a dozen aftershocks."

The homeowner is disturbed that he owes the bank more on his house than the house is worth. "A bad investment," the Jew tells him, "is like a spoiled puppy that requires even more attention than a baby. You learn to love it all the more."

The Jew tries a new bread knife. "The bread was never easier cut. But even this knife will not work for a good bagel."

The poet complains that the most recent book did not sell many copies nor receive any reviews. "Even if your book sold and was reviewed," the Jew says, "it would not have been able to compete with Schwartz or Goldberg. So at least you have avoided that disappointment."

The Jew sees a crab. It is an ordinary crab.

A hard worker has been summarily fired from a job, replaced by a person with less experience and less ability. "The person who did this," says the Jew, "will never understand the wrong that has been done and so will not be able to make amends. The only thing worse than what has happened to you has already befallen this person."

A man buys a suit on sale that is too tight at the waist and long in the sleeves. "Yes," says the Jew. "Things often turn out like this."

The lifeboat capsizes and the passengers are close to drowning. "I always wanted to be buried at sea," says the Jew. "But I had hoped to die on land first."

A tear graces Jesus's cheeks as he suffers on the cross. "That tear is not for his own pain," says the Jew, "but his pity for those who condemn any man to death, regardless of what he has done."

The waves wash over the child's magnificent sandcastle. The Jew consoles the heartbroken builder: "The castle will always be more beautiful in your memory than it could have ever been in the harsh light of the day. Tomorrow, the waves of your mind will erase even the memory of your castle. Making is its own best reward."

The patient does not know whether the treatment is more injurious to life than the disease. "Whatever you do, it is bound to be a giant, annoying, and irrevocable mistake," counsels the Jew. "So you might as well make the best mistake you can."

The young scholar cannot decide the best color for a new couch. "Pick not the color you want to see," says the Jew, "but the color you want to sit on."

Little hope is given that the cake will be ready for the wedding. The party planners are beside themselves. "An unfinished cake," says the Jew "is like a marriage in progress: tomorrow is always in the offing."

A business deal goes sour when the main investor runs off with the owner's spouse. "A fly in the ointment is the proof in the pudding," says the Jew.

A reader complains about the obscurity of a line of verse and seeks a Jew's counsel. "Obscurity is like the yeast in a cake. It is long acting to ensure the dough rises on time."

Vandals steal the pump's handles. "You think this is bad," says the Jew. "You should have seen the neighborhood before the vandals moved in."

A miller notices that the grain is too coarse to sell and is advised to consult a Jew. "Cohen still owes me 14 dollars."

A Jew writes a book in which he bears false witness against his friend, also a Jew. How could my friend turn against me? A Jew is asked for advice: "When Jew does this to Jew it creates a problem: it's harder to ascribe it to anti-Semitism. But not impossible."

A high-handed literary critic dismisses the irony in a work. The writer turns to a Jew. "The absence of irony in a work," says the Jew, "is like a window pane without a window: impossible to justify."

Two parents both claim a child is theirs. A Jew is brought in to arbitrate. "Don't try that ruse where you propose cutting the child in half," says one parent. "We weren't born yesterday," the other adds scornfully. "Yesterday's ruse is like a jackhammer drilling in sand," says the Jew. "The end result is still a hole in the ground."

The scholar cannot understand an unusual diacritical mark over a word in the text he is studying and ponders on it for several days before asking a Jew. "It means nothing," says the Jew, blowing a speck of dust off the page.

MANIFEST AVERSIONS, CONCEPTUAL CONUNDRUMS, & IMPLAUSIBLY DENIABLE LINKS

I love originality so much I keep copying it.

Immature poets borrow. Mature poets invest.

POETRY WANTS TO BE FREE. (Or, if not, available for long-term loan.)

I'm the derivative product of an originality that spawns me as it spurns me.

The work of art "itself" does not exist, only incommensurable social contexts through which it emerges and into which it vanishes.

The author dies. The author's work is born.

Poetry is a secret society hiding in plain sight, open to ear and mind's eye.

The shock of the new for some, the invigorating tonic of the contemporary for others.

A work of art is the overlay of a set of incommensurable possibilities, linked together around an anoriginal vanishing point.

CONCEPTUAL POETRY IS POETRY PREGNANT WITH THOUGHT.

(The absence of conception had itself to be conceived.)

THE POET IS A LIAR.

THE POET IS A LYRE.

THE POET'S TIRED.

(Poetry abhors a narrative.)

"I did not paint it to be understood, but I wished to show what such a scene was like."—J. M. W. Turner (1842)

L=A=N=G=U=A=G=E P=O=E=T=R=Y: a loose affiliation of unlike individuals.

Which reminds me of the story of the man who reports a wife-beating to a neighbor. "Then stop beating her," the neighbor replies. "But it's not my wife!," replies the good Samaritan, becoming agitated. "That's even worse!" says his neighbor.

No parodist goes unpunished because in these times the parodist is pilloried for the views he or she parodies. In a world of moral discourse absent ethical engagement, only the self-righteous go unrebuked.

I was born yesterday . . . and'll die tomorrow.

So What

This is so & so is this
But neither is important.
That is theirs
& near's not here
But neither is important.
Never twill, never twine
Nor peep nor bleat nor pipe.
Neither's important.

CARPE DIEM: CARP AND DIE.

I am not the man I was much less the one I will be nor imagine myself as, just the person I almost am.

A bird calls but I hear only its song.

My skin is burning but inside I am as cold as the North Pole. My shivering is metaphysical, a kind of involuntary davening.

Religion is giving religion a bad name.

Nor am I an atheist. I believe in the fallible gods of thought and in my resistance to these gods. I have faith in my aversion of faith.

Take care not to define yourself against others' belief systems. Their God does not define the domain of my profane, their Devil does not wash away my sins.

The water colors in watercolors.

I'm an observant Jew. I look closely at the things around me, as if they were foreign.

Sandy as a sugar donut, salty as a red rose . . .

You're either awake or asleep or will be.

I am not a secular man, but in moments of crisis I turn to agnosticism for the comfort it gives in freeing me from superstition. Once, when gravely ill and sure I would die at any minute, I embraced agnosticism, and, with Nietzsche in hand, swore I would remain an agnostic even if I recovered. But once I did recover, I lapsed again into religious belief, feeling the danger was over and it was safe to return to my old ways. Still, the fear of dying under the veil of dogma still grips my soul late in the night, and I yearn for the courage to embrace reality without prophylactics.

My mind is a labyrinth with well-lit exit signs; as much as I try, I can't ignore them. When I take leave of my mind I put myself in the care of my brain. In this way, I become again the animal to which my mind is blind.

There's no depth to the depth.

In the world of the imagination, impossible just means the next opportunity to get real.

The ceremony of sorrow is performed with a measured, defiant acknowledgement that makes words charms, talismans of the fallen world. Poetry is a holding space, a folded grace, in which objects held most dear disappear, returning as radiant moments of memory's forgiving home.

[for Akilah Oliver]

Turner's *sheerness.*

Existence needs essence the way a walking tour needs local color.

But a hole in an argument is not the same as a point of light.

Rather than an expression of love, justice is a protection against our inability to love.

We are most familiar with our estrangement; it is our home ground.

The absence of an accent is also an accent.

Yet the Dark, untouched by light, injures it all the same.

AND AENIGMA WAS HIS NAME, O!

Gather ye rosebuds while you can
Old times are locked in an armored van
Story's told, hope's shot
Chill out for the ultimate not

ARMED STASIS

I will make a fact with you Robert Frost.
Me on the one side, you on the one side.
No learned astrologer will ever
Separate us, crouching in the proverb-
Ial darkness even when it sounds like
Light.—Gosh I gotta go soon, even now
The Jersey shore beckons, my cabana
For your cheddar, my bootstraps for your boot.

UNREADY, UNWILLING, UNABLE

Peerlessly literal,

We're a little nearer than we were.

There is nothing I would rather see
than an angel dancing on a rhyme

or a unicorn playing Phaedra.

I love humanity; it's people I can't bear.

I am a Jewish man trapped
in the body of a Jewish man.
I love people;

humanity scares me.
If nothing is translatable, then

everything is.

Scars me.

Sob rule.

Boss is serrated.

Slush life. (The slope of the sloop is

spooked.

The revolutionary spectacle of a baby tearing off her diaper or a crippled young boy casting aside his crutches cannot help to move all those who yearn for liberation, a liberation that is blocked by the cruel forces of fate and biological inequality.

Poetry doesn't exist to be understood or to solicit accolades or dismissals.

It does what it does, what it can do.

When it comes it

comes, when it

goes it

goes.

This is the secret of rhythm.

For what leaves one person high and dry is for another as necessary as water. And can you have that necessity for one without at the same time sacrificing the availability to another? (And those two points of accessibility/inaccessibility may also occur for the same person at different times or even different parts of any one of us, odd as that may sound.) Poetry's power (*some* poetry's power) may be that its appeal is not universal but specific (not popular but partisan); we don't all agree.

If everything is translatable, nothing is.

)

Then I came to a pork in the road.

Mediocre politicians campaign in poetry and govern in prose. Great politicians campaign in prose and govern in poetry.

Camp is a drag.

Sometimes at night when I can't sleep I take down one of the volumes of my vast *Yellow Pages* collection. *Too much light.* So I go to "Draperies, shutters, and blinds." But which one? Draperies, shutters, or blinds?

I write to forget (or just

                                  not think

      about it

                 too much

).

There ain't nothing like a metaphor

                        nothing in this world.

       There ain't nothing you can name

               that is anything like a metaphor.

—Hold it. I gotta take this call. It might be from someone more important than you. (I don't even know you.)

Infinite joy in finite time; finite pain in infinite time.

My little blurb must think it queer
To stop without a poem book near.
But I have proverbs still to write
To shore me 'gainst frightening night.

Grenier: "*Green* in green shines."

nowhere now here ⁅⁅now here no where⁆⁆
[Ronald Johnson]

Time's loopy as a pretzel, salty as belly lox.

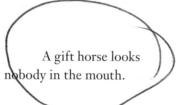

A gift horse looks
nobody in the mouth.

The more one turns away from a thing

the greater the force with which it returns

in the

unconscious.

Tea Party: I love America so much I want to lock her in my
basement to have her all to myself.
We've come to take

your country back. (O U R

AMERICA NOT

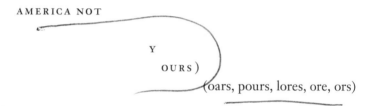

Y

OURS)

(oars, pours, lores, ore, ors)

Nothing is done forever or everything

is done forever. Poetry often operates
in the spaces
between intention &

serendipity. Or it reframes/displaces/
replaces *where* the intentionality

lies.

But how readers interpret the result of randomization is not random; we

project meaning, associate freely, symbolize the process/structure.
Who decides what poetry ought to be? Historically,

poetry's history suggests many radical swerves from
such *oughts* and of course much

compliance as well. What some reject as empty
others embrace as visceral. And what some
embrace as rational/sensible poetry others reject as

empty, lifeless.

Poetry's not about what it says but what it does.

"For where one finds commensurability with paraphrase, there the
sheets have not been rumpled; there poetry has not, so to speak,
spent the night."
[Mandelstam, tr. Brown]

So in the end what is comes down to is
Can the truth handle truth?

Wake up and smell the plasticine.

RECIPE FOR DISASTER

1 brown pillowcase
2 cans 20W20 motor oil
1 DVD *William Shakespeare's Romeo and Juliet* / *allusion*
2 pony tails *references*
1 1854 edition of *Leaves of Grass* ↑ *Whitman*
6 matching leatherette banquettes (beige) *also on*
3 sarcastic innuendos " *On Election*
13 nightingales *Romanticism* *Day* "
4 oil paint sticks (ochre)
∞ resignation
1 tube tanning oil

Play DVD chapter 3 in loop while grinding
Leaves of Grass with the innuendos. Soak
pony tails in motor oil and shake gently over
banquettes. Let motor oil sink in then apply
tanning oil by hand. Garnish with pillowcase
and paint sticks. Release nightingales.

AFTER LEMINSKI

My cut-off head
Thrown in your window
Moon-lit night
Window open

Hits the wall
Loses some teeth
Falls to the bed
Heavy with thought

Maybe it's scary
Maybe you'll blink
Seeing by moon
The color of my eyes

Maybe you'll think
It's just your alarm clock
On the nightstand

Not to scare you
Only to ask kindlier treatment
For my sudden head
Departed

CATULLUS 85

Hate and love. Why's that?, you'd ask
Don't know, I feel it and it's torture.

PSYCHOLOGY OF COMPOSITION (VII)

It's mineral the paper
on which to write
verse; verse
that is possible not to make.

Mineral are
flowers and plants,
fruits, animals
when in a state of words.

Mineral
the horizon line,
our names, those things
made of words.

Mineral, at last,
any book:
'cause the written
word is mineral, the cold nature

of the written word.

João Cabral de Melo Neto (1950)
translated with Horacio Costa and Régis Bonvicino,
after Djelal Kadir

VENEREAL MUSE

O Heart's Muse, you palace lover—
When January winds hover
Over dark despair of snowy night
Will you have heat to make blue feet white?

Will you bring life to marbled shoulders
With moonlight-pierced shutters?
Knowing money's spent and throat's dry
Will you harvest gold from azure sky?

Every eve you got to earn your bread
Like a boy in choir giving head
Blowing smoke to a God nearly dead

Hungry for tricks, you strut like a queen
Till your laugh, soaking in tears unseen
Jogs joy from a vulgar spleen

Baudelaire, "La Muse Vénale" (1857)

POEMS FOR REHAB

hang in
turn up
attune

. . . . .

silence
is
unnerving

. . . . .

who ?

God hurts those hurt themselves.

. . . . .

Vengeance is mine sayeth the ideological state apparatus.

. . . . .

just give me one more choice

. . . . .

be here then
be then there
be there now

. . . . .

hope is the thing
feathered with loss

WON'T YOU GIVE UP THIS POEM TO SOMEONE WHO NEEDS IT?

Remember what I told you about purgatory?
Limbo? How all that's happening now is just
this waiting around till the big cheese makes up
her mind about you? She makes you the way
you are and then decides if it panned out; for
every ten half-baked cookies there's a gem
&, you know, just maybe you're one of those.
Then there's those take her name in vain—
whaddya call them?—the religious moralists;
she don't much cotton to them, not when
they try to take away a woman's right to choose
or bad-mouth folks almost as queer as she is.
Well, everyone makes mistakes. That's what
purgatory's for. Sometimes it happens that
while you wait you see what's what—start
accepting you're in a long queue for God
only knows what. And neither of you has
any idea what the hell the matter is or what
to do about it.

THE MOST FREQUENT WORDS IN
GIRLY MAN

the
is
of
to
in
and
like
you
that
it
on
for
but
with
not
as
war
no
or
are
this
my
we
at
be
just
what
me
your
all
by

from
have
say
has
if
was
so
more
out
don't
when
one
there
they
up
then
let's
never
now
were
who
its
than
can
poem
way
into
only
been
time
bricklayer's
every
get
our
before
over

arms
after
go
I'm
which
will
even
other
going
people
right
see
would
can't
how
know
about
any
back
first
his
man
still
I've
nothing
off
world
had
long
oh
without
again
always
do
down
he

here
make
take
these
think
day
end
two
us
where
away
come
heart
lost
nor
their
those
till
am
face
line
part
same
thought
could
her
life
many
name
things
wrong
between
blue
home
painting
red

around
find
got
left
mean
own
show
some
something
song
them
yet
you're
another
art
becomes
call
each
hold
human
moment
much
new
place
there's
too
well
while
against
almost
also
behind
better
give
heaven
middle

mistake
money
next
seems
street
truth
water
work
being
bird
days
door
double
fire
form
green
hard
hope
look
love
may
orange
should
that's
word
break
change
else
eyes
girl
girly
hand
horse
inside
keep
let

men
mind
must
near
old
promise
she
subject
touch
turn
under
want
why
action
anything
didn't
fear
feel
getting
great
guy
head
hey
hiding
house
light
made
most
myself
neither
once
person
reality
says
school
shadow

shot
sky
such
through
today
told
TV
walking
accident
anyway
boat
book
bridge
center
comes
cry
did
eating
ever
further
God
good
ground
Jew
least
lighter
little
live
maybe
mother
night
poetry
put
said
side
social

someone
stand
start
stop
tears
used
what's
woman
won't
years
across
because
beyond
boy
contemporary
cut
death
doesn't
edge
enough
far
feeling
few
fog
frame
hear
hidden
image
isn't
it's
liberty
lose
making
meaning
morning
please

poems
point
political
possible
rather
read
reading
real
rights
saying
shadows
sign
sing
state
sure
understand
until
very
west
year
ago
air
allowed
beauty
become
beginning
big
blank
borders
brighter
broken
came
cannot
child
color
count

course
dance
dead
dear
everyone
everything
extension
fall
feelings
fighting
final
forest
four
full
goes
greatest
gurly
hit
ill
language
later
less
looking
loss
matter
mine
need
notice
ocean
outside
parts
perhaps
publisher
road
shop
shows

silence
sleep
small
smell
station
stealing
sun
sway
taken
takes
taking
talk
they're
thing
though
three
took
totally
trade
trying
violence
voice
walk
wave
working
wouldn't
write
yourself

DEATH ON A PALE HORSE

Circumstance guards way before
Targets long out of reach but forever
Emblazoned on mind's horizon.
Like phase or water without wetness
Sheer incline to other slope
So that shibboleth becomes
Token of last year's dope
Or cagey proportion not quite sized
For the next reason. How completely
Dandy, doing dithers in slivered
Solicitude or postcoital entropics.
Seize the tone or time'll
Trick every last one of you, it's
That close, that final.

Look up in the sky, it's a
mercurial representation
of things in themselves, the
action not the doing,
the done not the lunge.
Dr. Kildaire in his mythopoetic
struggle with Ben Casey;
the crown tools; shop
shock. Killer patois bisects
nominalization ratio at too
frequent a clip. Vividly
vacuous—though you probably
think that's something to aspire
to. Glow don't gorge, except
on alternate news days. There
are floats in them harbingers.
Bust a truss.

CHARON'S BOAT

Unsealed in its concealing, the *I*
Merrily rolls its *r*'s and minds its
Q's, a ways away from falderal
That names a place in line for
Godliness of views. The sump
Pump's low on expiating power
As all the shimmers parlay bets
That blank'll blight the probe of
Next week's trenchant, pensive
Slump. Stubble along pleats &
Stumbled plies of done done that
(don't do that). Nickel's worth of

IF YOU SAY SOMETHING, SEE SOMETHING

for Emma

It didn't happen that fast
clobbered by the silt of mineral movement
tempted to board the welter
of inspecific media capture
burnt like leers on the sprain.
Cajole me into oblivion if not
obliviousness, clotted clearings that
jam like slate. I didn't
mean to do it—intention
doesn't even enter the equilibrations.
Send me away, I've never been there.

10 December 2008

["TOMORROW, DAWN . . ."]

Tomorrow, dawn, when the countryside's almost white
I'll depart. You see, I know you're waiting for me.
I will go by the mountains, I'll go by the woods.
I can't be faraway from you anymore.

I will be walking with my eyes fixed on my thoughts,
Without looking around, without hearing a sound,
Alone and unknown, with back bent, with my hands crossed,
Sad, and the day for me will be like the night.

Then I won't look at the golden evening, so grave
Nor at the faraway sails veering toward Harfleur
And when I do get there, I will put on your grave
A green holly bouquet and flowering heather.

3 September 1847

Victor Hugo, Les Contemplations *XIV*

TODAY IS THE LAST DAY
OF YOUR LIFE 'TIL NOW

I was the luckiest father in the world
until I turned unluckiest.
They shoot horses, don't they?
In the mountains, the air is so
Thin you can scarcely say your
name. I dreamt I was a drum.
In the dream, I dreamt I was a
school boy afraid of school. I dreamt
I was drowning. Far away, the
crush of snow refracted the still muted
light. As if punishment was not
punishment enough.

14 January 2009

TIME SERVED

Honor her voice in me. Where
want knows neither hope nor deceit.
Flown, as if bent in place or
smacked into temporary adjust
filter after total system flush,
revamped by best-in-view anchorage.
Just salty enough, goes
on where the instigations to
instantiation are plumb zero,
bearish on fate, bullfrog
of a guy, no spills. Argument
ages past warrant. Funhouse
carbonization. Folded into lore.

Honor her voice in me. And still
a searing can be seen. Under adequate
convocation, the apparatus collapses on
cue. Far more than would be
impingement. I grieve, in tow,
untie by stalling, as honor
lives by two, habits accent
by holding steady, a lifeboat to
nearly everything. Bridges buckle
weathered to their climate. I
feel as if the days done gone
and left me in this
lone and fearsome blind.

SYNCHRONICITY ALL OVER AGAIN

It would always begin by not
being there, hiding behind the lot
that just sold for twice the reserve—
as in echo will get you bounce,
pouncing to the growl of faded
tunics flayed on the piano by
old-time losses and newly garnered
spools. I put this disc on before
but it never sounded like this,
sounded like you cared, sounded
like the ache in artichoke or the
service at a schul. Don't even go
there, we've been over that
a trillion times, and I still don't
see how this connects, how
you expect that I would
understand, or even go full
fathom for your lugubrious
form of wit. *It would always
begin that way*, as if you'd
heard it without listening,
somewhere in the inner spaces
of your disattention, the only
place paradise has been known
to coalesce, just moments before
the rent is dew.

LE PONT MIRABEAU

Under the Mirabeau bridge flows the Seine
    And our love
  Comes back to memory again
Where always joy came after pain

      Comes night, the hours sound
      Days go round in which to drown

Hand in hand, face to face
    While underneath
  The bridge of our embrace
Eternal gazes, weary waves

      Comes night, the hours sound
      Days go round in which to drown

Love goes away like the water flows
    Love goes away
  Like life is slow
And like Hopefulness is violent

      Comes night, the hours sound
      Days go round in which to drown

Pass the days, pass the nights
    Neither time past
  Nor love comes back
Under the Mirabeau bridge flows the Seine

      Comes night, the hours sound
      Days go round in which to drown

Apollinaire, Alcools *(1913)*

MORALITY

so what
so what
so what I'm
what I'm saying
so what I'm
so what I'm saying
I'm
I'm
I'm saying
it's
it's
it's
it's your
it's
it's
it's
it's your fucking
it's your fucking
it's your fucking fault
fault
it's your fucking
your fucking fault
fucking fault
I
I
I
I don't
I
I don't
I
I don't need

don't need to hear
hear
I don't need to hear
don't need to
don't need to hear
to hear
hear all
all
all
all
that
all that
don't need to hear
all that extra
all that extra stuff
stuff
I don't need to hear
all that extra
all that extra
all that extra
all that extra
all that extra stuff
stuff
all that
extra stuff
so that's
that
so that's
that's
so that's
so that's it
it
that's it
so that's it
it
that's it

so that's it
I don't
I
I don't
I don't need
I
I
don't need
don't need to hear
all that extra
extra stuff
all that extra
extra stuff
it's
it's
it's
your
it's your
it's your
your
fucking fault
your fucking fault
fucking fault
it's
it's
your fucking
your
your fucking
your fucking fault
it's your fucking fault

THE INTROVERT

after Wordsworth

Suddenly, those fears
Your first and ever-dreaded foe! Suddenly
You turn from some imbecile prose
That rails and ricochets against chimeric life
With dictums ripped from surface
Scars by wanton brains, a moral pose
Thoughtlessly ill fit to Orphic lyre
And with your beauteous breath you slowly
Refuse refuge, jolting yourself with jeers
That anxious years will bring an empty heart
And blinded thought.

STRIKE!

Strike because the sky turns gray just before it blacks out.
Strike because when you were little your father told you too many
lies.
Strike because the surf is up.
Strike because you are heartsick with the old ways and giddy with
promise.
Strike because things can't go on this way any longer.
Strike because the thugs have replaced the thugs.
Strike because every grain of sand tells you the universe is an open
field of infinite possibility.
Strike because you're sick & tired of bait & switch.
Strike because the wolf howls in the garden's translucent
masquerade.
Strike because your grief overwhelms you and the other option is to
sit at home and stare at a screen.
Strike because every hope begins with disappointment.
Strike because the bosses need a reality check backed up by workers'
sweat.
Strike because collective action is the only thing that separates us
from pejorocracy.
Strike because you're not for sale.
Strike because the sun is not shining as brightly as it did.
Strike because the machinery of greed needs to be unhinged.
Strike because you've lost your head in the endless circuits of a
recurring nightmare.
Strike because your children insist it doesn't matter and your
parents say the time's not right.
Strike because even demons are mortal.
Strike because the ache is just too bad, the work too much, the
reward too meager.
Strike because you have no say.

Strike because it wasn't supposed to be this way.
Strike because the pilots are guiding the ship to the plutocrats' lair.
Strike because every assault needs to be countered, every affront acknowledged.
Strike because you're hungry for something else.
Strike because you can't forget it and are not going to let it pass.
Strike because your dignity is worth more than their hypocrisy.
Strike because hands are for making things not wringing a desperate man dry.
Strike because power is a two-way street with back alleys, overpasses, byways, and unexplored tunnels.
Strike because your only hedge fund is your bare hands.
Strike because the coal dust is suffocating and the mines a living grave.
Strike because you are sick of all that's called new and despair that nothing changes.
Strike because you are abandoned.
Strike because you don't want to live this way anymore.
Strike because the deck is stacked but the dealer says you're cheating.
Strike because everyone's listening but no one's talking.
Strike because you can't say it any other way.
Strike because meaning's made not taught.
Strike because life's a tale and you the teller.
Strike because I told you to.
Strike because I will never let you down.
Strike because I told you one thing but did another.
Strike because I disappointed you.
Strike because I made you feel stupid for trying.
Strike because I made you feel stupid for crying.
Strike because, win or lose, it's the doing that gets done.
Strike because you couldn't get a ticket to the show.
Strike because you've never had a thought of your own.
Strike because no one bothered to tell you.
Strike because you still can or think you can or thought you could.
Strike because it's better than baseball.
Strike because tomorrow they'll come for you.

Strike because this could be your last chance.
Strike because even though you have your price, the offer was not
nearly good enough.
Strike because resistance is happier than humiliation.
Strike because you'd prefer not to.
Strike because eternity is ours for the asking.
Strike because the wind is at your back, even when there is no wind.
Strike because all roads lead nowhere and all hopes come to naught,
at least if things don't get worse.
Strike because the jellies in your life are lined up at tide's edge,
keeping you from the water.
Strike because you are thirsty and the water is spoils.
Strike because even a match in a dimly lit restaurant can make it
easier to read the menu.
Strike because you hate the way they redecorated the planet.
Strike because the fall season needs some push back.
Strike because your wrongs are not as bad as their wrongs.
Strike because you forgot to pay attention for longer than you'd
intended.
Strike because the bells are ringing but you are nearly deaf.
Strike because you would have when you knew less than you think
you know now.
Strike because the blood loss can't be sustained.
Strike because you heart is broken and the vultures are overhead,
ready to pick at the pieces.
Strike because complacency's a waste of time.
Strike because while doing something is a pain in the ass, doing
nothing is a pain in the soul.
Strike because a shadow of a doubt is the hipster's swan song.
Strike because you didn't when you could and now it's too late.
Strike because it's noisy.
Strike because it's bluesy.
Strike because there's not enough poetry in your life or it's the
wrong kind of poetry.
Strike because you're running on empty.
Strike because the nightingale's restless.

Strike because the meds are kicking in.

Strike because you are in love or've lost your love, are on a roll or've hit a dry spot, are out of ideas or brimming with plans, breaking down or working out.

Strike because the wealthy would rather you die than pay their share of taxes.

Strike because we criminalize poverty and legalize corporate theft.

Strike because the men at the top are not the top men.

Strike because you used to believe in America or never did but wanted to.

Strike because the Supreme Court is jerry-rigged, its justice without honor.

Strike because Murdoch and Berlusconi make Big Brother seem like chopped liver.

Strike because it's no fun to tango alone.

Strike because you've been on hold for longer than you can remember and want to hang up without losing your place in the queue.

Strike because it's nearly as effective as Prozac.

Strike because there is not enough orange in your green or mauve in your magenta.

Strike because the Manhattans are tasting sour and the gin rummy's flat.

Strike because it's futile.

Strike because no one cares what you do.

Strike because you mean it or meant it or isn't it pretty to have thought so.

Strike because I told you you wouldn't want to hear this and you don't.

Strike because you want a break, or you've been broken, or you've seen the larger picture, or your vision is deteriorating and you can only see what's right in front of you.

Strike because in order to fully appreciate sitting sometimes you got to stand.

Strike because in the end even dreams turn to sand.

Strike because you didn't think you had it in you.

Strike because you don't have it in you.
Strike because the iron is cold and as heartless as the green ant's misery.
Strike because you missed the revolution.
Strike because the revolution comes only twice in each one's life.
Strike because the revolution is not an end but a meeting.
Strike because your apathy brings you infinite joy.
Strike because you've lost your voice.
Strike because you have the choice.
Strike because you want to join the chorus.
Strike because you've always wanted a solo.
Strike because it's taking too long.
Strike because you want to sing this song.

SAPPHICS

Here where I found you, here will I lose you
Tears on the slow take, tears on the up swing
Hidden when I go now, crushed by a token
Sorrow as a cancer, reason eschews answer
Mobbed by a gay light, scarred in a queer fright
Little did I know then, nothing do I ken now
Fate is a torn wing, hope is a hypocrite.

RECALCULATING

You can't be part of the problem if you don't see how you're part of the solution.

"For a poem is not the Poetic faculty, but *the means* of exciting it in mankind."
[Poe, Drake-Hallek review]

Information wants to be free—from personification.

As if all we are and do revolves around a hollow center.

Every poem is a model of a possible world that only comes into being when reading is active, activated.

The poem is a constant transformation of itself.

As in the poem plays you or you play the poem. Aces are witches, clubs beat the rhythm, spades are queens, and kings rule!

We didn't have it when we needed it but got it once we didn't.

Postmodernism: modernism with a deep sense of guilt.

Language is an albatross, a sullen cross, a site of loss.

I think of Emma climbing the icy rocks of our imagined world and taking a fatal misstep, one that in the past she could have easily managed, then tumbling, tumbling; in my mind she is yet still in free fall, but I know all too well she hit the ground hard.

The hardest thing is not to look back, the endless *if onlys*, the uninvited *what could have beens*. I live not with foreknowledge but consequences; wishing I had foreknowledge, suffering the consequences of not.

. . . how poems become sites for mourning—not in fixed ritual repetitions (prescribed liturgy) but as mobile and specific areas for reflection and projection, holding areas, havens. Not words received for comfort but works actively discovered in the course of searching.

Not to "get over" (as a disease) but as a way of "living with" (as a condition).

The nightmare reality that erupts in the daylight like burnt offerings at a pizza parlor. You say skeleton, I say: *Can you say that again?* That's no phallus, that's the election of my impotence, writ large. As in: *Me transformo*, you pale face. *Me tranformo*, you the unexpected product of a sudden revelation.

I love art so much . . . but it never returns the favor.

Poems are stuck in black and white, which means that every color connected to a poem is proof of the inner life of words.

As surely as God invents the idea of God but also of godlessness.

Angels brush against spattered brushwork, gory purple eyes loom out amidst hearts pierced by arrows.

Every misfigured thought a dialect of its moment. *(Say! Don't you speak in a dialect too?)*

Sometimes I am disturbed even by my ability to function. I feel, at times, a shell of myself, a shell of a shell of myself.

Each day I know less than the day before. People say that you learn something from such experiences; but I don't want that knowledge and for me there are no fruits to these experiences, only ashes. I can't and don't want to "heal"; perhaps, though, go on in the full force of my dysabilities, coexisting with a brokenness that cannot be accommodated, *in the dark.*

Right after Emma died I could not stand to look at the photos of her—and there are lots, because she made so many self-portraits. I felt each photo was a lie—flaunting her presence in the face of her being gone. Now I see that the photographs are what she left me— that she is present to me in the way these haunted and haunting works are present.

Whale on beach like wolf at wedding: bark is bigger than bite but insulates tree.

[For Yunte Huang, after Charlie Chan]

Poetry should be silent, unread, invisible, inconceivable. The true poem can never be written or heard.

Not ideas but the idea of ideas; not questions but the inadequacies of answers; not currency but *against the tides.*

Better a weak jaw than an iron fist.

Stalling is my inspiration.

It's what I'd like to undo that keeps me up at night.

The problem with teaching poetry is perhaps the reverse of that in other fields: students come to it thinking it's personal and relevant, but I try to get them to see it as formal, structural, historical, collaborative, and ideological. *What a downer!*

Orphaned by the world, with no home but there.

If you don't make a mistake thrice, how do you learn from it?

If x is x, then y is y and o, o.

So much of what we can't imagine we are forced to experience. And even then we can't imagine it.

I've got a chiasmus as big as all Detroit and as old the Second Avenue el.

He had the honeyed lips of someone who'd been in poetry too long, whose idealism had years ago become a manner of speech and whose only aesthetic aspirations were for a revival of the ideas he had rejected in his youth, as if you could get a second chance to bite the apple of the new and not come out smelling like a candied turkey in a slow dance medley. It was a fork in the road, but he had always favored spoons; and now, facing the music to which he had never dared to listen, he dove into the waters he has always reviled, ready to be eaten alive by the sharks of his proudly arrogant misjudgments.

This is the difference between a sentence and paradise. A sentence comes to an end; paradise has no beginning.

China export: "NOT MADE IN CHINA" T-shirts
US export: "NOT MADE IN AMERICA" T-shirts

It was the kind of day you read about in the movies.

What's unseen but said's as consequent as what's apparent but unspoken. Words perform for inner eye we o'erlook at pleasure's peril.

Listening for inaudible songs in a sonic sea, I lost my bearings, falling, uncaring, into traps of my own despairing.

Always treat advice with skepticism (especially this advice).

Freedom from ideology's ideology's designer jeans.

Ideology's veils are imaginary; the freedom from these veils delusional.

Universalism is moral, particularism ethical.

(But every apple has a core, every horizon a philosophic song . . .)

We are gathered at a site of dialogue. As chaotic as our discussions may sometimes seem, we are always making patterns with them.

Most of those patterns are lost in the dark matter of the mystic writing pad.

When I say "we" I don't mean everyone, or perhaps anyone else, just a sense of some collectivity beyond myself.

"We aced the shit out of that asshole."

My advice to young poets is always: start your own magazine or press and publish your own work and those of your contemporaries whose poems seem most crucial for the art, as you perceive it. And respond as much as possible, through poetics and reviews, to this work. Articulate its values; value its articulations. The web certainly makes such publishing easier, but it does not solve the hardest part, finding a community of other poets that allows for active and intense exchange, not based just on location or prior friendship or like-mindedness but on the qualities and quiddities of the work as it unfolds in time and space, on earth and in the heavens of our "image nations."

Our inalienable rights are inevitably alienated; in this way, capitalism seems to merge with destiny; or our fate, through a darkened glass, is projected onto the world of which we are sentient.

So then it's necessary to be reminded, from time to time, that hegemony is something to work for rather than only and ever to recoil against.

I've grown so accustomed to the dark that I can hardly imagine anything more than shadows.

The Jew is a textual construction.

You're not there even when you're there.
You're not gone even when you've went.
You're still near even when you're gone.

In poetics, nothing is new except the exaggerations.

Beauty lies, I have always thought; a wonderful deception while it lasts.

The Beach trilogy (a family saga over three generations): *Seagull with Broken Wing, Rocks in Basket, Shadows in the Sand.*

Elliptical poetry: language poetry's bark without its bite.

The absence of ornament is an ornament.

Robin's "Wandering Jew or Nomad," cut from the leather back of his family's Salt Lake City rocker: valuable more for what it is than to look at it. But isn't that true of all of us? (Something to touch amidst the loss.)

Here's the message: *there is no message.*

I'm talking to you, you motherfucker.

You want a message, go to a massage parlor.

I hope I have your attention now.

Your message has been scrubbed because of possible contamination by a virus.

"A highly concentrated state of intoxication—a state which, like madness, frequently enables the victim to imitate the outward demeanor of one in perfect possession of his senses."
[Poe, Pym]

It's always darkest at night. A darkness day can't touch.

But we learn to live with it or anyway it learns to live with us.

Think snow and see Boca.

Crane is not metrical so much as parametrical.

My palsied heart and I agree . . .

It may be impossible but the concept is that we articulate our judgments, preferences, and beliefs while being aware that these are not universally shared; this holds a special problem for those whose beliefs include a belief in the universality of their beliefs.

The cause of the cold is not the cold.

We live facing the blinding sun of the not-yet born, in the shade of the dead. Meaning is the liminal space where the dead live in us as we look toward the future.

"It is all very confused but more confused than confusing."
[Stein, *To Do: A Book of Alphabets and Birthdays*]

"Shadow, come, and take this shadow up."

Are we here yet?

For now, I go hour to hour . . .

If you are not part of the problem, you will be.

MISFORTUNE

after Nerval's "El Desdichado"

My morning star's dead and my disconsolate lute
Smashes in the blackened sun of torn alibi.
In the tomb of every night, memories of
Venetian reveries raw rub the inconsolable
Pitch of the dark, where over and again
I love you.

BE DRUNKEN

Be always drunk. That's all: that's the only question. So not to feel the horrific heaviness of Time weighing on your shoulders, crushing you to ground, you must be drunken ceaselessly.

But on what? On wine, on poetry, or on virtue, in your fashion. But drunken be.

And if sometime, on palace steps, on the green grass by an abyss, in mournful solitude in your room, if sometime you awake, drunkenness dimmed or done, ask of the wind, of the wave, of the star, of the bird, of the clock, of all that flees, of all that wails, of all that roils, of all that sings, of all that speaks, ask what hour it is and the wind, the wave, the bird, and the clock will answer: "It is the hour to get drunk! So not to be the slavish martyr of Time, be drunken; be drunken without stopping! On wine, on poetry, or on virtue, in your fashion."

Baudelaire, "Enivrez-vous" (1864)

Dun forgot t' til me
what I din fer you afore
all the 'ittle nuthin
we flooked in'ide the or.
Dun forgot the whisters
that I never known y'had—
the intessant gloopy ghlisters
'ost in squamush seas of plaid.
Nah, don't forget the worgy blays
or the foomish 'urple blain—
then I acomin' 'ome ag'in
you'll never known I 'ent.

CHIMERA

At dusk I found it silent there
And sudden caught it in my hand
It squeaked and hollered with despair
But I was young of ruthless mind.
I scooped and cupped it in my palm
So it would no more come to harm
Yet quick I knew to let it go
It was not mine to have nor hold.
E'er since that day I've gathered twine
To knot and glue unto a rime
Resigned that tunes will never bind
Shimmering shadows tossed in time.

BEFORE YOU GO

Thoughts inanimate, stumbled, spare, before you go.
Folded memories, tinctured with despair, before you go.
Two lakes inside a jar, before you go.
Flame illumines fitful lie, before you go.
Furtive then morrow, nevering now, before you go.
Lacerating gap, stippled rain, before you go.
Anger rubs, raw 'n' sweet, before you go.
Never seen the other side of sleep, before you go.
Nothing left for, not yet, grief, before you go.
A slope, a map, insistent heave, before you go.
Stone & stem, nocturne, leap, before you go.
Compass made of bones & teeth, before you go.
The wind up acts, delirium's beast, before you go.
Spilt quell, impatient, speaks, before you go.
Rippling laughter, radiance leaks, before you go.
No place, no sound, nor up, or down, before you go.
Smokey, swollen seeps, before you go.
Tossing in tune, just like last night, before you go.
I'm nowhere near the fight, before you go.
Nothing to make it right, before you go.
It won't congeal, no more deals, before you go.
Hope a fence, well's on fire, before you go.
Slammed when you don't, damned if not, before you go.
A hound, a bay, a hurtled dove, before you go.
Coriander & lace, stickly grace, before you go.
Englobing trace, fading quakes, before you go.
Devil's grail, face of fate, before you go.
Suspended deanimation, recalcitrant fright, before you g
Everything so goddamn slow, before you
Take me now, I'm feelin' low, before yo

Just let me unhitch this tow, before y
One more stitch still to sew, before
Calculus hidden deep in snow, befor
Can't hear, don't say, befo
Lie still, who sings this song, bef
A token, a throw, a truculent pen, be
Don't know much, but that I do, b
Two lane blacktop, undulating light

NOTES & ACKNOWLEDGMENTS

Some of these poems were originally published in *Aerial, Baffler, Barrow Street, Blackbox Manifold, Boog City, Caliban Online, Cimarron Review, Claudius App, Coal Hill Review, Columbia Poetry Review, Conjunctions, Critical Quarterly, E. G. Reader, Electronic Poetry Review, Esque, Fulcrum, Golden Handcuffs, Green Integer Review, Half-Circle, Harper's, Hobo Magazine, International Literary Quarterly, Island Magazine, Journal of Interdimensional Poetry, Lingo, Lyric &, MiPoesas, NO, Non, Onedit, Plume, Poems & Poetics, Poetry, PoetsArtists, Prague Literary Review, Prairie Schooner, Rampike, Sentence: A Journal of Prose Poetics, Shampoo, Tikkun, Vallum, Vertaallab, Virginia Quarterly Review, Vlak, War & Peace, Weekday,* and *Work.*

Recalculating includes my translations of poems by Velimir Khlebnikov, Osip Mandelstam, Charles Baudelaire, Guillaume Apollinaire, Régis Bonvicino, and Catullus. These translations were collected in *Umbra,* a pamphlet from Charles Alexander's Chax Press (Tucson, AZ, 2010). "Umbra" was originally published in *Content's Dream: Essays 1975–1984* (Los Angeles, CA: Sun & Moon Press, 1986). "I've been given a body . . ." (from *Stone*) and "To empty earth falling unwilled . . ." were written for *Modernist Archaist: Selected Poems by Osip Mandelstam,* edited by Kevin Platt (Miami, FL: Whale and Star Press, 2008), and were also published in *Shofar.* Some of the other translations were published in *S/N: NewWorldPoetics* and *New American Writing.* Thanks to the heirs of João Cabral de Melo Neto for permission for the translation of "Psicologia Da Composicao," from *In: O Cão sem Plumas* (Rio de Janeiro, Brazil: Alfaguara, 2007). "After Leminski" is a collaboration with Bonvicino.

Some of these poems were included in *The Introvert* (Paris: Collectif Géneration, 2010), with accompanying pictures by Jill Moser, Yang Yongliang, Carlos Amorales, Jiři Čirnický, and Dominique Figarella; each artist made twelve copies of the book.

"All Set" was included in *100 Poets against the War*, edited by Todd Swift (Cambridge, UK: Salt Publishing, 2003).

"Before You Go," with pictures by Susan Bee, was published at artcritical .com (2011).

"Breathtails" is a libretto written for Anne LeBaron, scored for baritone, shakuhachi, and string quartet. It was commissioned by Thomas Buckner.

"Brush Up Your Chaucer" was written at the invitation of David Wallace and presented at the Contemporary Poets Meet Chaucer panel at the New Chaucer Society's Conference, Fordham University, at Lincoln Center, summer 2006. It was published in *Hotel Amerika* 6, no. 1 (spring 2008).

"Catullus 85": Richard Tuttle suggested we work together on translating the much translated "Odi et amo. quare id faciam, fortasse requiris. / nescio, sed fieri sentio et excrucior." The possibilities included: "Hating & loving. Query: why'd I do that? / Don't know, just sense it & it's excruciating" and "Odious & amorous. Hey: why'd I do that? / Beats me, just feelings & I've been crucified."

"The Importance of Being Bob" written for the Bob Perelman feature of *Jacket*, no. 39 (2010), edited by Kristen Gallagher.

"In Utopia" was first published in the *Occupy Wall Street Poetry Anthology* (New York: Occupy Wall Street Library, 2011).

"Ku(na)hay" was included in *Best American Poetry 2008*, edited by Charles Wright (New York: Scribner's, 2008).

"Lenny Paschen Redux" is a recasting of the monologue for *The Lenny Paschen Show*, the libretto for a 1992 opera with music by Ben Yarmolinsky, collected in *Blind Witness: Three American Operas* (Queens, NY: Factory School, 2008).

"Not on My Watch," while not written for this context, was selected by Franklin & Marshall College to be part of a public arts project adjacent to the Shreiner-Concord Cemetery, Lancaster, Pennsylvania, commemorating the grave of radical abolitionist and civil rights advocate Congressman Thaddeus Stevens.

"Recipe for Disaster" was written for the Suzanne Bocanegra recipe issue of *Esopus* (2010).

"Talk to Me": On April 18, 1999, I performed this improvised poem as part of Deb Singer's "Impulsive Behavior" series at the Whitney Museum's Philip Morris space. Also on the bill that night were Edwin Torres and Bruce Andrews performing with Sally Silvers. A video of the performance is available at PennSound (http://writing.upenn .edu/pennsound/x/Whitney.php). The text was first published in *Fulcrum* 7 (2011), with a response by Dubravka Djurić.

"A Theory's Evolution" was published in the Philadelphia *Inquirer* (Dec. 29, 2006), with the title taken from a recent *Inquirer* headline about a Darwin show at the Franklin Institute in Philadelphia.

"Todtnauberg" was published as part of an essay, "Celan's Folds," in *Textual Practice* (2004).